# Crisis and Care

# Crisis and Care

*Meditations on Faith and Philanthropy*

EDITED BY
Dustin D. Benac and Erin Weber-Johnson

*With a Foreword by* Craig Dykstra

CASCADE *Books* • Eugene, Oregon

CRISIS AND CARE
Meditations on Faith and Philanthropy

Cascade Books
An Imprint of Wipf and Stock Publishers
199 W. 8th Ave., Suite 3
Eugene, OR 97401

www.wipfandstock.com

PAPERBACK ISBN: 978-1-7252-9789-0
HARDCOVER ISBN: 978-1-7252-9790-6
EBOOK ISBN: 978-1-7252-9791-3

*Cataloguing-in-Publication data:*

Names: Last, First. | other names in same manner

Title: Crisis and care : meditations on faith and philanthropy / Author Name.

Description: Eugene, OR: Cascade Books, 2021 | Includes bibliographical references.

Identifiers: ISBN 978-1-7252-9789-0 (paperback) | ISBN 978-1-7252-9790-6 (hardcover) | ISBN 978-1-7252-9791-3 (ebook)

Subjects: LCSH: subject | subject | subject | subject

Classification: CALL NUMBER 2021 (print) | CALL NUMBER (ebook)

To the caregivers:

You have held us on the edge of uncertainty.
You have met us in our deepest moments of crisis.
Making meaning out of chaos, you now carry us over with
hopeful imagination.

# Table of Contents

# Contributors

Thad Austin, Senior Director of Strategic Initiatives and Congregational Engagement at the Ormond Center for Thriving Congregations and Communities, Duke Divinity School

Eric Barreto, Frederick and Margaret L. Weyerhaeuser Associate Professor of New Testament, Princeton Theological Seminary

Dustin D. Benac, Visiting Assistant Professor of Practical Theology, George W. Truett Theological Seminary, Baylor University and Louisville Institute Postdoctoral Fellow

Amy Butler, Founder, Invested Faith

Sunia Gibbs, Artist, Activist, Pastor

Dave Harder, Parish Properties and Parish Collective Canada

Shannon Hopkins, Co-founder and Lead Cultivator RootedGood

David P. King, Karen Lake Buttrey Director, Lake Institute on Faith & Giving, Indiana University Lilly Family School of Philanthropy

Aimee Laramore, Owner/Lead Consultant for ALlyd Image Solution and Philanthropic Strategist, PhD Program in African American Preaching and Sacred Rhetoric

Emily Hull McGee, Pastor, First Baptist on Fifth

Patrick Reyes, Senior Director of Learning Design, Forum for Theological Exploration

Mark Sampson, Co-Founder and Lead Learner, RootedGood

Mieke Vandersall, Owner and Principal Consultant, Vandersall Collective

Erin Weber-Johnson, Senior Consultant, Vandersall Collective

Trey Wince, Executive Vice President for Ministry Incubators and Staff Consultant for Ministry Architects

Kevin Kim Wright, Chief Programs Officer, Urban Arts Initiative

# Foreword

I CAME TO KNOW most of the authors included in this fine book when they participated in one of the four-year-long programs that Leadership Education at Duke Divinity offered to a diverse community of leaders of a wide range of Christian religious institutions. We called the program *A Convocation of Christian Leaders.* The members included pastors of congregations, professors in theological schools and church-related colleges, leaders of a wide variety of kinds of denominational agencies and faith-based social service agencies, and lay leaders whose manifold gifts were ready to be put into play. The idea was to create a sense of community among representatives from the many diverse streams of Christian faith and practice from all across the United States.

It worked! Christian institutional leaders from all across the country have come to know one another and to draw on each other's gifts, talents, perspectives, connections and resources. And they continue both to keep in touch with each other and to deepen their relationships. Many of them spend significant amounts of time in one another's institutions and collaborate in supporting one another's efforts. And perhaps most importantly, both the editors and a number of the other leaders who participated in the early convocations have written for this fine book as well.

*Crisis and Care* builds on that foundation. It does so, however, in a world that has changed radically. We live in a context of pandemic. And so, as Aimée Laramore points out in her chapter,

"Emergency Bag$ in Crisis," our time calls for "a laser focus on innovation and impact to meet unprecedented needs."

This wonderful book is full of gems. Take a look at Patrick Reyes' beautiful essay, "Grandma's Table." Or Emily Hull McGee's, "Bricks and Mortals: Sacred Spaces and the Faithfulness of Letting Go." Think deeply for a while with Kevin Kim Wright about "The Generosity of Death" and find your own reflections and practices of caring and giving transformed. Read "Seeing Our Rooted Good: Trees, Pandemics, and Economic Imagination" by Shannon Hopkins and Mark Sampson. It's brilliant. And the list goes on for a total of fifteen compelling chapters.

The editors' "Introduction" for this book tells us that now is a time to take risks. It is, indeed. And this book is calling us to do so in a variety of different arenas and contexts. Above all, it is calling us to live in "God's economy . . . one built on abundance, possibility, and constant re-creation." So read this whole book—section by section, chapter by chapter. Reflect on it with care and ask yourself what it is calling you to do. Find friends, neighbors and colleagues to read it along with you and create ways to bring your special gifts into play with others who are eager to do so with you.

Grace and peace be with you all.
*Dr. Craig Dykstra*
*Emeritus Professor of Practical Theology, Duke Divinity School*

# Acknowledgments

THIS VOLUME IS A collective effort that reflects the kind of generosity and mutuality that distinguishes Christian philanthropy. A Convocation of Christian Leaders, hosted by Leadership Education at Duke Divinity School, catalyzed our collaboration as editors and our connections to many of the contributors listed in this volume. We wish to express our gratitude to Craig Dykstra, Dave Odom, Gretchen Ziegenhals, Victoria White, Donielle Cyprian, and Mary Floyd Page for their leadership and hospitality. When we began envisioning this collaborative project, we called two trusted friends and colleagues: Christian Peele and Kevin Kim Wright provided early encouragement that shaped the trajectory of our work. David King and Jill Duffield read and offered gracious feedback on the Introduction and Conclusion. Our editor at Wipf & Stock, Charlie Collier, provided guidance at each stage—from the proposal to the final editorial work—in order to bring this project to completion. We are grateful for Charlie's shared vision for this project and Wipf & Stock's commitment to support publishing that enriches scholarship and communities of faith.

Our authors gave voice to our early vision to capture the kind of imagination that emerges where crisis and care meet. When we contacted them in the middle of a pandemic and mounting social crises, they responded with curiosity and candor. Like spring water in a dry land, authors' written meditations and engagement throughout the process revived our imaginations and rekindled hope. Working with and learning from our authors provided a source of great joy amid uncertainty; thank you for trusting us with your words and for supporting this collaborative effort.

We both wish to express gratitude for the contributions of our co-editor throughout this process. It is a humbling, but deeply rewarding task to learn from one another. As a scholar and practitioner, we were motivated by a shared understanding of the importance of partnership. As co-editors we worked together in a way that sought to perform the kind of collaboration that can renew and release new imagination.

I (Dustin) want to express my gratitude for several individuals and communities who shaped my understanding of faith and philanthropy. To Jack Burns, who provided my first introduction to the world of fundraising and proposal development. To Debbi Speck, a trusted guide and champion for more years than I can count; thank you for introducing me to the world of faith and fundraising and then teaching me to navigate this convergent space. To Abi Riak for graciously letting me learn from the wisdom drawn from decades of development experience around the globe. To Dan Struble, who served as a thoughtful conversation partner and colleague at key junctures in my development as a fundraiser and as a scholar. My work with Kate Bowler, Katherine Smith, and the Everything Happens team in the belly of this pandemic coincided with the inception of this volume; thank you for giving me my first shot. And to Craig Dykstra, an extraordinary doctoral advisor who nurtured the intellectual and institutional conditions where this collaborative work could take form.

Two Deans supported this work: Greg Jones at Duke Divinity School nurtured an environment that supported my training as a doctoral student and time as a Postdoctoral Associate. Todd Still at Baylor's George W. Truett Theological Seminary graciously provided time and institutional space to support the final stages of this work. Thank you for the way you each care for the broader ecclesial ecology where faith forms and education takes place.

To a broader intellectual community of doctoral students at Duke University; it is a rare space where kindness and curiosity coincide. To The Lake Institute on Faith and Giving's Theology and Economics Reading Group; a special thanks is due to Robert Saler and Elizabeth Lynn for facilitating an environment to explore literature that intersects with this volume. To Duke's Sanford School of Public Policy, Center for the Study, who provided a dissertation fellowship that allowed me to consider the intersection of faith and philanthropy. To David King and Brad Fulton, whose invitation to work as a qualitative researcher for National Study of Congregations' Economic Practices provided an opportunity to listen to pastors navigate the complexities of faith and congregational finances across the country. To the Louisville Institute, whose generous Postdoctoral Fellowship created time complete this project at a critical juncture.

Dan and Dianne Benac sowed the seeds of a hopeful imagination that finds form through the generosity; thank you for nurturing the language of faith. Finally, to my wife, Casey, your enduring support, love, and care created the space where these words and this work could take form. You embody the creativity and hopeful generosity that marks this work, reminding me each day how much better we are together. And to our children, Cade and Ellie, your presence and playfulness give me daily reasons to find joy. May the wisdom offered here give you a reason to continue living a life marked by generosity.

I (Erin) am reminded of the famous Rumi quote, "If you can only say one prayer in a day, make it thank you." In this way, I offer prayers of deep gratitude for those who have mentored me and informed this work. For Kevin Pearson, my first Episcopal Priest, who not only demonstrated how to raise funds faithfully, but paired it with a lifechanging theology of giving. For mentors Jane Butterfield and Titus Presler who affirmed my calling as a practitioner, sharpened my writing with care and patience, and daily taught me invaluable lessons for ministry. Jim Murphy who recruited me from Wagner Graduate School of Public Service at NYU to work at the Episcopal Church Foundation and provided regular guidance and support for nearly ten years. Thank you, Terri Mathes and Maurice Seaton, for your work as mentors to root the work of fundraising as a ministry. To Matthew Heyd who, as my supervisor in the grants department at Trinity Wall Street, challenged us to think critically about philanthropy. For the past five years it has been a privilege to work with Project Resource Faculty: Mike Orr, Shay Craig, and Betsy Jutras. Their work to provide contextually based stewardship resources is the type of collaborative innovation that inspired this book. My colleague and a contributor for this volume, Mieke Vandersall, deeply challenged my own money narratives and, as a result of our work together, changed the trajectory of my vocation. Mieke, your work inside and outside of institutions has charted new courses for so many! Mike Kinman, thank you for taking a chance on a young adult and recruiting me to serve on the board for Episcopalians for Global Reconciliation many, many years ago. I continue to be challenged and inspired by your witness in the world.

Judy Miller, these are days that are marked by courageous witness. You've beautifully embodied this courage in the midst of the ongoing crisis of the pandemic. Mike Angell for modeling for me philanthropic, collaborative leadership at its best! Derrick McQueen for challenging and reframing what I thought I knew about race and money—and doing so with abiding patience and love. Larissa Kwong Abazia, thank you for reading and rereading the chapter on philanthropic redlining and lending your wisdom. Devon Anderson, for your continued mentorship and brilliant guidance. I still rely on your words of counsel and advice. Stephen Hagerty who, as a colleague and guide, wonderfully turns each conversation into an opportunity to ask about one's walk with Jesus. Holley and Eric Barreto, friends, conversation partnerships and models of care in the midst of crisis. Courtney Veszi, my sister, for your consistent example of generosity and care.

Thank you to my parents, Craig and Beverly Weber who deeply formed me, as a child of God, for this good work. For my own saints, my sons, Jude and Simon Henri. One day, you will carry our family's stones of how we "crossed over." May one stone be the story of my unchanging love. Finally, and always, to my favorite husband, Jered. Each day, like every new endeavor, begins and ends with my thanks for your love and partnership.

In this moment, when it felt like the world was turning upside down, the individuals and communities named here provided harbors for hope. Their words, wisdom, and presence rekindled our belief that another way is possible, even in the wake of unthinkable crisis. We offer our edited work back to you, as an expression of care, with the hopeful expectation that the Spirit of God will continue to draw us together where crisis and care meet.

# Faith and Philanthropy

*Where Crisis and Care Converge*

DUSTIN D. BENAC

ERIN WEBER-JOHNSON

*"[W]e are groping our way toward the creation of new images."*
MARIA HARRIS, *TEACHING & RELIGIOUS IMAGINATION*

*"But when the fullness of time had come,*
*God sent his Son, born of a woman..."*
GALATIANS 4:4 (NRSV)

CRISIS RUPTURES OUR LIVES and remakes the way we inhabit the world. For many individuals and communities of faith, the interlocking social-ecclesial-political crises of 2020 marked a site of social and ecclesial rupture through experiences of collective vulnerability, uncertainty, and unrest. As Eric Barreto notes in this volume, it is a time that "laid bare truths to which prophets among us had been pointing for generations." For some, the pandemic feels like the unraveling of time, an unshakeable encounter with uncertainty that renders us unable to imagine future possibilities. For others, the pandemic brings with it expanded possibilities, an invitation to work for and implement change that has been envisioned for years.

Two images clarify the devastating and far-reaching consequences of crisis: flood and famine. Crisis can come like the waters of a flood. Like water spilling through a breached dam, the collective traumas of this moment wash over us with unrelenting force. Just as floods do not affect all equally, the flood of this crisis leaves some untouched. For others, however, this moment falls with cascading force. Those who were already standing in the gap for their families and communities. Immigrants. Entrepreneurs. Artists. The poor. The elderly. For many, this type of crisis may come suddenly, but it only grows without a known end. And as crisis heightens, we face difficult choices: leave or wait it out? Pack our bags or protect what we have? Care for others or care for ourselves? For some, our lives and communities feel flooded. Flooded by a deluge of crippling news. Flooded by grief that we cannot shake. Flooded by the memories of those we will never get back. As the waters reside across our flooded lives, we'll begin to assess what has been lost, trying to pick up the pieces of lives, dreams, and memories that cannot be remade or rebuilt.

Crisis can also come like a famine.[1] While some crises come suddenly, like a flood, others slowly build. We sense the fragility that surrounds us. We carry inherited burdens from those who came before us. We know the arid places of our lives and communities that leave us feeling cracked, without reserves, and dreading what may come next. But as the crisis deepens, these isolated sites of vulnerability spread, driven by the incalculable cost of famine, burdens gradually consuming our remaining reserves. Like a mounting famine, the interlocking crises of this moment slowly

---

1. Scott Kisker first used the term "famine" to describe this pandemic time (Spirit and Truth, "Pandemic Perspective: Reflections from Two Church Historians.") Kevin Watson kindly directed us to this language.

eat away at an already-meager subsistence that sustained our lives, work, and communities. In its place, many find themselves in an arid social-ecclesial-spiritual space. Separated from so many we hold dear and unable to gather as we once did, we face the aridity of isolation. Displaced from our ecclesial communities or unable to worship as we once did, we face the aridity of broken community. And left to pursue and practice an embodied faith in digital domains, we face the aridity of spiritual anemia. While some may escape the sudden waters of a flood, the crises that come like famines leave collective traumas. They mark our lives and communities in such a way that they become part of the story we tell.

While our individual experience of these interlocking crises differ, they constitute a rupture of our collective imagination. And, in its most basic form, this crisis of imagination affects the manner in which we inhabit time and place, including our neighborhoods, our communities, our congregations. Far from a siloed or sector-specific disruption, this disruption ripples through our social fabric that constitutes an imagination, refracting the manner in which we imagine and pursue a common life. As Dave Harder notes later in this volume: "We face a crisis of imagination."

Faith and philanthropy are a place of convergence between the interlocking crises we face and the formation of imagination. In the aftermath of COVID-19, with a heightened sense of vulnerability, economic uncertainty, and collective unrest, we, as editors, sensed two interrelated phenomena: (1) communities are uncertain about how to respond to the challenges they face and (2) money marks the imaginative horizon about how individuals and communities imagine what is possible. To borrow language from Maria Harris, "We are groping our way toward the creation of new images."[2] Amid the disparate experiences of this moment, philanthropy constitutes the fulcrum for imagination as individuals and communities consider what is possible in the wake of this rupture.[3] Money, as it acts in and through philanthropy, structures

2. Harris, *Teaching & Religious Imagination*, 5.

3. For a helpful discussion of the relationship of rupture, conversion, and theological reflection, see Bretherton, *Christ and the Common Life: Political*

our lives and communities of faith. Like the water we swim in, we readily participate in communities that are ordered through the interconnections between faith, finances, and philanthropy, but their precise influence is often hiding in plain sight. The economic consequences of this moment are considerable. This rupture may also provide an invitation to imagine and create alternative economies to support communities and people of faith. These varied expressions where crisis and care converge share a fundamental feature: faith and philanthropy intersect in ways that organize collective efforts to order a common life.

While local communities of faith and those who serve them are the primary focus of this volume, their philanthropic work remains connected to broader civic life. Mark Chaves concludes his 2017 assessment of the trends in American religion by noting: "If half of all the social capital in America—meaning half of all the face-to-face associational activity, personal philanthropy, and volunteering—happens through religious institutions, the vitality of those institutions influence more than American religious life. Weaker religious institutions could mean a different kind of American civic life."[4] For scholars of religion, philanthropy, and those who inhabit this network of religious nonprofit organizations, these trends and the attendant challenges that confront religious nonprofit organizations invite a reassessment of the social structures, philanthropic practices, and forms of leadership that guide the individuals and communities that gather in and around a changing religious sector. As communities of faith contend with this moment of rupture, philanthropy provides a point of convergence between the life of faith and a broader civic life.

Money, as religious studies scholar Devin Singh observes, is a medium that crosses boundaries between sacred and profane.[5] In moments of crisis, when our lives and communities feel flooded and we face the aridity of famine, philanthropy is an adjacent site to reimagine how we resource, organize, and imagine a common

*Theology and the Case for Democracy*, 28–29, 155–157, 330–332.

4. Chaves, *American Religion*, 121.

5. Singh, *Divine Currency*, 91.

life. People of faith are marked by time. As faith communities and those who serve them discern the marks of this particular moment of crises, the voices and stories gathered here mark this spot of time in a way that bends our imaginations toward Christ's incarnate possibility. In the face of flood and famine, their words and wisdom point to a form of ecclesial imagination that we carry with us as we cross over to the other side.

## Crisis and Care

The kind of imagination that rises to meet flood and famine emerges at the intersection of crisis and care. Drawing upon more than two decades of combined work in fundraising, philanthropy, and academic research, we wagered that a new kind of imagination is emerging, if we could only find the right voices to name it. Without denying the depth of crisis, this moment is brimming with adaptive possibility. We sensed the possibility for innovation, creativity, and care, even as the communities we inhabit, study, and serve strain under the gravity of this moment.

So, we doubled down on our bet and, as editors representing both academia and practitioners, sought to collaborate outside of our traditional peer circles. Rather than watching and waiting, we wagered that if we could gather the right voices, their words could help us discern the particular kind of wisdom and philanthropic imagination that is at hand. In this moment of grave crisis, we wagered that care was rising to meet the needs of individuals and communities.

We purposefully attended to the broader ecclesial ecology where the negotiation of faith and philanthropy is taking place in this moment. By 'ecclesial ecology' we mean the constellation of identifiable forms of organized, ecclesial life, such as congregations, theological schools, Christian colleges and universities, philanthropic centers and nonprofit, including experiments of creative deviance in the boundary spaces between existing and emerging orders. Innovation emerges at the points of contact between different members of an ecclesial ecology and the ongoing work of God in and through communities of faith.[6]

Just as the interrelated crises of this moment are not sector-specific, care is emerging across a broader ecclesial ecology. Accordingly, we invited contributors from established institutions as well as those who serve or work on the edge or beyond established institutions. We wanted to mark the ways crisis affects established organizations as well individuals who serve beyond existing institutional orders. With faith and philanthropy as a common concern, this volume attends to the points of shared imagination between disparate—and frequently siloed—expressions of organized religious life. Through the conversations moderated here, their combined words mark ways that care rises to meet moments of crisis within an ecclesial ecology.

## Defining Philanthropy

The meditations that organize this volume evidence decisive transitions in the ways communities of faith understand, pursue, and resource a common life. Oliver Zunz concludes *Philanthropy in America: A History* by pointing to the close relationship between the practice of philanthropy and the history of organizations in America. He writes: "Philanthropy in the United States is not simply the consequence of a universal altruistic impulse; it is also a product of the large organizational revolution that American managerial and financial capitalism orchestrated in the last century and a half."[7] While Zunz's historical assessment rightly contends that philanthropy in America cannot be studied without also examining the role of organizations, his work downplays the historic and ongoing importance of religion and religious organizations for philanthropy in America. Not only has philanthropy played a central role in "defining and sustaining numerous religious

6. Benac, "Adaptive Church."

7. Zunz, *Philanthropy in America*, 294.

traditions,"[8] but religious thought and practice has also motivated charity and philanthropy.[9]

This volume demonstrates how an imagination that is derived from the Christian tradition motivates philanthropy in the wake of crisis. The imaginations on display here demonstrate how this particular religious tradition animates authors' (trans)formative work, and how their contextual engagement reshapes their understanding of the Christian tradition. Like a double helix, faith and philanthropy move in a virtuous pattern of interrelationship.

Following the contributors to this volume, we define Christian philanthropy as *a way of life marked by generosity, including the ability to give to and be received by others, in order to enrich the common good.*[10] Attention to the intersection between faith and philanthropy provides a way to discern the wisdom that guides communities' historic and ongoing efforts to organize a common life. As described throughout this volume, faith leaders and their communities navigate this intersection in contextually-dependent manners across diverse organizational settings: a church plant in New York city reconsiders the money stories that surround their founding in order to move towards more sustainable mission-centered work; a vegan soup business provides a template for ministry beyond the full-time pastoral ministry model; an arts nonprofit reconfigures its annual funding gala in a manner that honors how meaning and messiness are conjoined for the people they serve; a philanthropic strategist, working with a PhD program to ensure all graduates are not bound with life altering debt, considers what needs to be left behind in this moment; social entrepreneurship emerges out of a new paradigm for connectedness; an entrepreneurial philanthropic effort invites sunsetting congregations to release the abundant resources they have to launch ecclesial renewal.

Four features distinguish this definition. First, Christian philanthropy is a way of life. Describing more than a technical

---

8. Ilchman, Katz, and Queen, *Philanthropy in the World's Traditions*, ix.

9. Hamilton and Ilchman, *Cultures of Giving*; Brooks, *Who Really Cares?*

10. See Tempel, Seiler, and Burlingame, eds. *Achieving Excellence in Fundraising* and Jeavons, *When the Bottom Line is Faithfulness.*

solution or programmatic outcomes, philanthropy describes a way of seeing and moving through the world. As such, it is a learned disposition that directs individuals' reflective and prereflective mode of engagement.[11] Second, generosity marks Christian philanthropy. Imitating God's kenotic form of being, Christian philanthropy is distinguished by its commitment to offer what one has for the sake of others. Third, Christian philanthropy includes the ability to give to and be received by others. This form of philanthropy requires mutuality, as expressed in the ability to offer and receive gifts from others,[12] within reciprocal relationships. Finally, philanthropy finds its fullest expression by enriching the common good. As a way of life, philanthropy emerges through participation in and connection to a local community. While faith communities' (trans)formative capacity remains indexed to local contexts, Christian philanthropy may support community-based change through its commitment to enrich the common good. In this particular moment, Christian philanthropy requires specific attention to testimony and acts of love in order to enrich the common good.[13] This final commitment rejects the zero-sum calculus that guides strictly economic approaches to community change, noting instead the latent possibilities that arise when we reimagine how to resource, organize, and fund a common life.

## The Power of Questions

After placing our bet, we asked fifteen of our trusted friends, guides, and conversation partners to join us as we tried to capture the wisdom of this moment. We invited each contributor to reflect on one or more of the following questions in relation to their particular context or area of expertise:

11. See Smith and Davidson, *The Paradox of Generosity.*

12. See Saarinen's *God and the Gift* for an insightful discussion of theology and the practice of giving and receiving.

13. Rolland, "How philanthropy and faith in diverse communities can guide us today."

1. Where do we see emerging theological expressions of giving, either within or beyond existing institutions?

2. How are leaders adapting approaches utilizing learnings from across institutions or, alternatively at the intersection of institutions?

3. What kind of wisdom guides adaptation? What sustains it? What needs to be left behind?

4. How do these expressions impact the institutional life? (i.e., inform, expand, limit, push the needle)

5. What resources, networks, and conceptual frameworks enable individuals to innovate within existing institutions and at and beyond the edges of institutions?

6. Are there previous moments of transition and uncertainty that can provide aids and inspiration for our current thought and practice about faith and giving?

As we discerned the kinds of imagination that arises when crisis and care meet, we presented these questions to authors in an invitational manner. We invited imagination instead of prescription. We wanted to discern—individually and collectively—what has been and is possible together.

The first question invites attention to emerging expressions of giving. With the broader ecclesial ecology in view, we invited contributors to help us see familiar spaces in new ways. Their responses identify emerging expressions of giving that cross conventional institutional boundaries.

The second question explores how leaders are translating insights across sectors. The interrelated crises of this moment have surfaced a range of adaptive expressions. Authors' responses describe their adaptive process, noting the importance of community, proximity, and collective discernment.

The third question identifies an organizing theme for this volume: wisdom. In the flood-like and famine-like crisis, wisdom guides individuals and communities forward. Authors' responses included both prophetic voices of what needs to be left behind in this moment as well as what ethical questions foster and guide individual and collective discernment.

The fourth question considers the impact of innovation on broader institutional life. As individuals across an ecclesial ecology respond to the challenges they face, this question presumes that change ripples through interconnected communities of faith. Responses identify the transformational impact of this moment and note what they are intentionally leaving behind.

The fifth question attends to the broader relational and conceptual matrix where crisis and care meet. We invited authors to help us map the landscape where innovation is taking place in this moment. Their responses combine descriptive and constructive insights to explore how philanthropy has historically organized their work, as well as the emerging possibilities.

The sixth question identifies previous moments of transition and uncertainty as sites to guide contemporary action. While a strictly chronological approach line of inquiry would begin with historical precedent, we intentionally inverted this order. Rather, we centered the crises of this particular moment in order to invite authors to interrogate previous moments in light of the current challenges they face.

## The Need for Meditations

We purposefully offered the genre of "meditations" to organize the various responses to these six questions. As intentionally short responses, each meditation presents a word on point, addressing contextually-specific concerns that arise from authors' particular work, ministry, or expertise. While we invited contributors to draw upon their research and scholarship, we also encouraged authors to write for readability. Their meditations display how matters of faith and philanthropy transcend the boundaries between our individual and institutional selves; rather, authors cannot describe the wisdom that is needed in this moment without first describing the wisdom that is derived from their experience. Drawing from this deep well, connection to a broader community of practice enables authors to translate the wisdom drawn from their experience to meet the needs of the communities they serve.

In developing the concept for *Care and Crisis,* we also intentionally set each presidential election of 2016 and 2020 as bookends for the project. Authors wrote each piece without knowledge of what the outcome of the 2020 presidential election would be as well as the timeline for the COVID-19 pandemic. Writing from a place of heightened uncertainty, the authors mark and name what we carry forward, what we leave behind, and the imaginative possibilities of this particular moment.

Certainly, there will be many publications that will analyze the years between 2016-2020 and, specifically the civil rights unrest of 2020 and the pandemic. What was striking, even prior to our physical distancing for many months in our homes, was the level of disconnection felt within faith communities, institutions, even families. Institutional silos created by titles of minister, academic, and practitioner were deepened in the midst of political, ecclesial, economic, and racial divides following the 2016 presidential election.

Our desire, in transcending assumed institutional structures, was to embody the collaborative and intersectional work we see emerging from this time of crisis. We intentionally invited contributors from established institutions and those working beyond traditional institutions. We invited authors from nonprofits and those who partner with nonprofits. We invited pastors of local congregations and those who serve as pastors to their communities.

The push and pull of individual meditations provide an accurate representation of the tension and opportunity of this moment. Their combined meditations bear witness to the work of imagination, of collaboration, and of care. In that embodying, our hope was to mark this moment—in all its uncertainty, fatigue, and possibility.

The meditations offered here can be read as an entire volume or individually. Even as we intentionally organized them to support a sustained argument, they can also stand alone. Their abbreviated format will enable institutional leaders, fundraisers, students, and pastors—each of whom regularly runs short on time—to read them in short sittings or between the many commitments that fill each day.

## Marked Time

Counting time marks Christian existence: Advent, Christmas, Lent, Easter, Ordinary Time. The rhythm of this time and the attendant practices pattern our lives and communities in ways that open us up to the reality and possibilities of God. When counted in the company of others, this pattern of time stitches our lives and collective imaginations together in ways that invite us to see the work of God in marvelous and ordinary spaces.[14] At the center of the story of Scripture, God comes to rewrite time. As the writer of Galatians notes, in "the fullness of time" (Gal. 4:4), God took on flesh; God rewrote time, imprinting our ordinary existence with the reality of incarnate possibility.

Even though our time is marked and counted, we move through time unaware. Like the silent ticking of a grandfather clock on the threshold, the gentle 'tick-tick-tick' becomes an ambient feature of our ordinary existence. Until the ticking stops. For many individuals and communities of faith, the interlocking social-ecclesial-political crises of 2020 disrupted our typical movement through time. Much as the incarnation rewrites time, crisis ruptures our lives and remakes the way we inhabit the world.

The year 2016 marked a tectonic shift in American life, culture, politics, and economics. With these larger cultural movements so followed a significant change in the fundraising landscape—change that has continued and deepened to the present moment. With religion historically being the largest recipient

14. Edie, *Book, Bath, Table, and Time.* As Edie writes: "Understood in this way, the *ordo* constitutes a living communal ecology: one that included initiating persons into Christian faith through baptism (bath), then continued to nurture them in faithfulness through their baptismal callings through sustained participation in the book (Bible), table (Eucharist) and Christian timekeeping" (7).

of charitable dollars in the U.S.,[15] a dramatic shift in philanthropy has a noticeable impact on faith communities, religious institutions, judicatories, and parachurch organizations.

This volume examines how disruption, starting with the General Election of 2016 and following, impacted the landscape of faith-based philanthropy. Studying donor motivations provides one site to consider how the landscape has changed. Following the 2016 election, and the campaign cycle that led up to it, new donor motivations emerged, giving trends changed dramatically, and the charitable tax law went into effect. Along with nonprofits and charitable organizations, the church is continuing to grapple with the new reality of these seismic changes.

Since the election in 2016, advocacy-based organizations on both sides of the political aisle have seen significant increases in giving. The ensuing four years saw a dramatic increase in "rage donating," with individuals directing their dollars and their donations toward whatever they perceived to be the latest outrage, attempting to regain some sense of personal agency through the act of giving. If it is true that our philanthropic giving testifies to what we believe and shapes how we act, then this was never as true as in the past few years, with philanthropy becoming a means through which Americans increasingly made their voices heard and their impact felt. With fears and animosity amplified, fundraisers, like politicians, discovered that people can and often will donate as a means of expressing not only their ideals, but their outrage.[16] In late 2016 and early 2017, as the newly formed Trump administration began to ensconce campaign rhetoric into policy, advocacy groups sought to connect donors' needs with philanthropic opportunities.

With the landscape changed, old patterns and assumptions about philanthropy are in need of continual testing and revising. Yet, in the face of disruption, the leaders in this book from both inside traditional and non-traditional ministry contexts, as well as the institutions that support and partner with faith communities

---

15. Giving USA, "Giving USA 2019: Americans gave $427.71 billion to charity in 2018", lines 72-73.

16. Teson, "Rage Donations," para 1-2.

(philanthropic organizations, seminaries, academies, faith-based nonprofits, etc.) reflect on emerging theological expressions of giving.

This variety of contexts and perspectives, both inside and outside religious institutions, is intentional. We believe that the wisdom necessary to navigate the shifting ground of fundraising in our present moment has and will continue to come from the convergence and interaction of seemingly disparate sectors. When philanthropy is seen as ministry, when gifts are given for the work of repair of the world and for the work of being reconciled with God and neighbor, then lives are transformed.

As with any ministry, adaptability is always needed to meet the emerging needs of donors. Just as leaders of faith-based organizations were finally unlocking how to fundraise in ways relevant to the post 2016 reality, the ground continued to shift. As organizations tapped into these newly realized donor motivations, increasing giving, and attracting first time donors, they were now faced with a perennial fundraising challenge of how to persuade these new contributors to continue giving. The "Trump Bump" became an exercise in how to move individuals from reactionary giving to ongoing, intentional support.[17]

When the COVID-19 pandemic happened, it brought mass unemployment and market volatility. In this context, COVID-19 disrupted the world. With it, countless predictions were made as to the economy. Unemployment rose as individuals lost their jobs or were unable to work due to lack of childcare and/or becoming ill.

Many nonprofits worried the disruption would keep them from engaging in needed fundraising. Many have drawn parallels between this present crisis and the Great Depression. Interestingly, an unexpected parallel between now and that former time of great economic uncertainty and precarity, is that like now, charitable giving actually increased during the Great Depression. In fact, *The New York Times* reported on December 8, 1931 that giving to 155 Community Chests (predecessors in many cases to United Way

---

17. Joslyn, "Trump Bump." para 1-3.

organizations) rose some 14.9% between 1930 and 1931.[18] The 1950 Sage Foundation report also indicated that charitable giving increased overall in 1931.[19]

Similarly, many faith-based communities and organizations are seeing upticks in giving. In a recent Evangelical Council for Financial Accountability (ECFA) study,[20] 47% of responding churches reported increased giving in April compared to both last April and January of 2020. An additional 25% of churches said giving in April was about the same as January. A Greater New Jersey Conference of the UMC study revealed that year-to-date giving among their churches is improving, with 54% of churches seeing giving growing or holding steady, compared with 50% in April.[21] Both the ECFA and UMC study indicated that the majority of churches are optimistic about their financial futures.

And in the midst of economic uncertainty, Americans bore witness to the police killing of George Floyd in Minneapolis, yet another instance in a long litany of violence and injustice toward Black Americans. Our country is still reeling with the after effects. As a result, millions more white Americans are waking up to the full story of inequality and racism in our nation.

As donor motivations are shifting, studies of Philanthropic Redlining detail the inequality that exists on how grant dollars and donor dollars are given to nonprofits.[22] Those with Black, Indigenous, and Persons of Color (BIPOC) serving in leadership roles were granted significantly less funding than institutions led by white leaders. Indeed, not only is funding less, but often funding that is provided comes with burdensome additional criteria to fulfill.[23] As more Americans become aware of inequity, there

---

18. Andrews, *Philanthropic Giving, 50-68.*

19. Andrews, *Philanthropic Giving, 50-60.*

20. Bird, Warren. *Covid Financial Report. 7-8.*

21. United Methodists of Greater New Jersey, "Weekly Survey Results," lines 35–39.

22. Rendon, *"Nonprofits led by people of color,"* para 1-10.

23. Rendon, *"Nonprofits led by people of color,"* para 12.

has been an intentional focus on giving to organizations led by BIPOC, displaying givers' desire for agency as well as passions.[24]

The Presidential election of 2020 will signal new donor motivations and with it—new disruptions to the system. We are now seeing, after years of stasis, a speeding up of church closures. Leaders in churches are seeking other places to serve and use the wisdom they've gained. In short, changing trends in philanthropy evidence the unique ways crisis and care converge in this moment.

## Overview for this Volume

The five parts of this volume develop an argument about the wisdom that is emerging in the rupture of crisis. Specifically, it marks the forms of possibility that are emerging in this moment, locating the site for new imagination where crisis, care, and philanthropy meet. As communities of faith navigate ongoing challenges, this volume speaks to the type of imagination that rises to meet the specific crises of this moment, even as authors' words may give hope and guidance in future times of need. Like the development of a musical fugue, each section shares the central theme of this volume, but they develop it according to an organizing topic. When combined, the contributions across this volume follow a similar pattern and intersect in ways that enrich the collective conversation. Like the preached word offered to the congregation, these various contributions find their final form when they resonate together in the context of a broader community. This simultaneously collective, imaginative, and contextual engagement points to the wisdom that can continue to sustain communities in the space between crisis and care.

Part I, "When the Field Changes," marks the ways the landscape has shifted around faith communities. Intentionally starting with two practitioners, this first part purposefully locates the complexities of this moment at the local level. Drawing upon their combined ministry and time guiding ministry leaders, the

24. Hill, "28 Organizations," lines 6-7.

contributions to this section name what we are leaving being. Aimée A. Laramore invites ministry leaders to leave behind ingrained markers that guide ministry: the church as building; the connection between generosity and in-person worship; our collective ability to "outperform" racism, fragility, and vulnerability. As Laramore notes: "Although the pandemic was a new paradigm in these ministry conversations, crisis was not." Trey Wince suggests we are leaving behind the full-time ministry model for small-scale ministry. David King proposes these interlocking crises invite leaving behind the assumption that we can approach matters of funding and philanthropy without also considering "the moral nature of philanthropy and the pluralistic visions of the public good." Without ignoring the loss that leaving things behind entails, these contributions share a hopeful optimism marked by new questions and the emerging possibilities in this moment of change. As Wince notes: "Like it or note, desperation prompts innovation, and the table is set for both."

Part II, "Innovation: At the Intersection of Crisis and Care," considers how innovation emerges when crisis and care meet. Offering the wisdom from his Grandma's table, Patrick Reyes names how memories of survival offer an alternative imagination that subverts dominant narratives of adaptation. Reyes's meditation also performs the alternative vision he narrates, inviting those who carry the wisdom of their grandmas' tables to "step[] into [their] power in this moment" and those who carry the wisdom of a dominant culture to learn to sit and wait at a reconstituted table. Thad Austin directs attention to the role of collaborative partnerships as a site to renew ministry "in a post-pandemic world." Drawing upon six years of research, Austin names the transformative promise of collaborative partnerships as pastors and local ministry leaders form bonds of trust, mutuality, and mutual support. Emily Hull McGee concludes this section by describing how the "faithfulness of letting go" can guide communities as they repurpose and reimagine their sacred spaces. Written as pastor of a historical mainline congregation in North Carolina, McGee describes how her congregation made the decision to tear down many of their beloved structures that marked a previous era of cultural prominence. Combining this narrative with a scriptural imagination, McGee demonstrates how grief and innovation carried this shared work forward: "Time and time again, when we found ourselves caught in the grip of an identity crisis, God's enlivening Spirit beckoned us relentlessly to hear the ancient promise echoing throughout time and space: *I am about to do a new thing; now it springs forth, do you not perceive it?*"

Part III, "From Barriers to Opportunities," marks this moment by exploring how the perceived barriers of this moment have become opportunities that invite new imagination. Kevin Kim Wright notes how a fear of death translates into our organizational life. Ironically, as Kim Wright notes, "Christians are no stranger to death and yet, when given the chance, we take every opportunity to avoid it." Even as the interlocking crises of this moment bring the stench of death, Kim Wright describes how his arts nonprofit in New York received this moment as an invitation to approach fundraising in digital domains as a way to expand their community and reflect the particular experience of the people they serve. Dave Harder questions the dominant narrative that centers church buildings as the contextual center for worship, community, and religious leadership. Without denying the importance of buildings or ignoring the complexities of change, Harder's words are neither naive nor sanguine. Rather, he invites us to receive and tell "stories that reflect a new imagination for our buildings" with the hope that we can "leverage[] the asset of real estate for sustainable mission." Shannon Hopkins and Mark Sampson's co-authored piece questions the "economic master story" that privileges autonomy, competition, and the zero-sum logic of scarcity. In its place, they direct our imaginations to see "the relationship between things as the core fabric of reality" by drawing wisdom from the interconnected character of trees. As Hopkins and Sampson note, the movement from barriers to opportunities requires a reorientation in what and how we see, offering salve and sustenance for "our weary institutional imaginations."

Part IV, "Crisis and Care Embodied," includes three case studies that develop the themes from this volume in contextually-specific manners. While each meditation in this volume attends to the complexity of context, these three meditations explore how examining the relationship between faith and philanthropy has renewed local thought and practice. Erin Weber-Johnson tells the story of the Collective Foundation, which marks an institutional response to the legacy of philanthropic redlining. As Weber-Johnson notes, institutionalized expressions of redlining inform the philanthropic sector as well, requiring BIPOC communities to "work twice as hard for half as much." Mieke Vandersall presents the case of St. Lydia's, an entrepreneurial church plant in Brooklyn, New York. Written as a ministry partner and guide for this community, Vandersall describes how this small, scrappy congregation moved towards sustainable witness by examining the money stories that surrounded their collective work. As Vandersall concludes, when these money stories are untangled, they invite us to bear witness to the "newness [that] is consistently being woven amid the rubble of the world around us." Finally, Amy Butler describes the vision of Invested Faith, which aims to embody a theology of abundance through philanthropic entrepreneurship. Rather than being blinded by the loss and decline that marks some communities of faith, Butler invites sunsetting congregations to see the possibility that emerges when they choose to "invest[] in the future of faithful witness in the world." The meditations in this section imagine and embody an alternative economy that can meet the needs of communities in this moment.

Part V, "Reimagining Wisdom on the Edge of Certainty," explores how crises extends an invitation to new imagination. While imagination is a consistent theme throughout this volume, these concluding meditations identify sites that can fuel an imagination about faith and philanthropy. Utilizing Acts as a source for inspiration, Eric Barreto considers how a scriptural imaginary "nurtures an imagination in us about faithful belonging." As contemporary communities work to nourish more life-giving community, Barreto identifies three insights in Acts that can fuel alternative imaginations: (1) Difference is a gift; (2) Community is a matter of life and death; and (3) The empire is crumbling from within. Sunia Gibbs's meditation identifies how new imagination emerges when our work combines a willingness to experiment and the vulnerability to utilize strengths outside of dominant narratives. Writing as a pastor and an artist, Gibbs performs a kind of imagination that receives an invitation to innovation in the particular intersections that mark our lives and communities. Dustin Benac concludes by describing the wisdom that emerges when we attend to the broader ecclesial ecology where crisis and care meet. Drawing upon his research in the Pacific Northwest, Benac suggests new imagination may emerge when we consider how ecclesial ecologies provide a *place* for formation, constitute a *prism* that refracts imagination, and are enriched by a *philanthropic vision* that supports the conditions for new imagination to form and flourish.

## An Invitation

As we write, we linger in a time of uncertainty and waiting. We await the arrival and distribution of a vaccine. We await the return to some semblance of normalcy. We await the conclusion of a prolonged election season. We await a return to Ordinary Time. The lines of the Advent hymn, O Holy Night, provide a fitting description: "The thrill of hope, the weary world rejoices / For yonder breakers, a new and glorious day." Indeed, in this not-yet moment that currently marks our lives and communities, we look, with hope, to a new and glorious day.

We are also mindful that this particular moment merely discloses what has always been true about our communities: they are at once more fragile, more resilient, and more beautiful than we could ever imagine. This reality has marked our own lives during the season of our writing. Personal transitions. Moves. Covid diagnoses. And abundance of care from our families, colleagues, and communities. Even as the various contributions bend our imaginations toward hope, we cannot easily forget the feelings of disruption, uncertainty, and loss that mark our individual and collective lives in this moment. We feel it in our bones.

Even when crisis is less palpable, the meditations of this volume offer an invitation: amid the flood and famine of crisis, let us look for and kindle new imagination. Uncertainty is not foreign to communities of faith, even as we wish to avoid it. Though we will want to forget it, the wisdom drawn from this moment can bear us forward. As we listen and learn together, care may rise to meet the various crises we face. In the midst of uncertainty and change, it is vitally necessary, while paying attention to disruptions, to learn from innovative leaders that work across sectors. This constant connection across institutional lines is the foundation for all adaptation. Specifically, it is imperative that we work in collaboration, creating space for voices across academic, congregational life, and the nonprofit sector to reflect on faith and philanthropy.

As we mark this time, we remember we belong to one another. This reminder, this constant in the midst of change and cultural divisiveness, describes both human need and organizational adaptation. It is fitting then, in belonging, we grow and learn.

*Advent 2020*
*Dustin Benac, Waco, TX*
*Erin Weber-Johnson, St. Paul, MN*

## Bibliography:

Andrews, F. Emerson. *Philanthropic Giving.* Russell Sage Foundation, 1950.

Benac, Dustin. "Adaptive Church: A Practical Theology of Adaptive Work in the Pacific Northwest." ThD diss., Duke University, 2020.

Bird, William E. *Optimism Outweighs Uncertainty: Covid-19 Financial Income Report.* Winchester, VA: Evangelical Council of Financial Accountability, June 2020.

Bretherton, Luke. *Christ and the Common Life: Political Theology and the Case for Democracy.* Grand Rapids: Eerdmans, 2019.

Brooks, Arthur. *Who Really Cares?: The Surprising Truth About Compassionate Conservatism.* New York: BasicBooks, 2007.

Chaves, Mark. *American Religion: Contemporary Trends.* 2nd edition. Princeton: Princeton University Press, 2017.

Edie, Fred. *Book, Bath, Table, and Time: Christian Worship as Source and Resource for Youth Ministry.* Cleveland: The Pilgrim Press, 2007.

Giving USA. "Giving USA 2019: Americans gave $427.71 billion to charity in 2018 amid complex year for charitable giving." https://givingusa.org/giving-usa-2019-americans-Gave-427-71-billion-to-charity-in-2018-amid-complex-year-for-charitable-giving.

Hamilton, Charles and Warren Frederick Ilchman. *Cultures of Giving: How Region and Religion Influence Philanthropy.* San Francisco: Jossey-Bass, 1995.

Harris, Maria. *Teaching & Religious Imagination: An Essay on the Theology of Teaching.* San Francisco: Harper & Row, 1987.

Hill, Zahara. "28 Organizations That Empower Black Communities." *The Huffington Post.* February 17, 2017. https://www.huffpost.com/entry/28-organizations-that-are-empowering-black-communities_n_58a730fde4b045cd34c13d9a.

Ilchman, Warren, Stanley Nider Katz, and Edward L. Queen. *Philanthropy in the World's Traditions.* Bloomington: Indiana University Press, 1998.

Jeavons, Thomas. *When the Bottom Line is Faithfulness: Management of Christian Service Organizations.* Bloomington: Indiana University Press, 1994.

Josylyn, Heather. "'Trump Bump' Still Lifts Fundraising for Many Charities." *Chronicle of Philanthropy.* January 17, 2018. https:www.philanthropy.com/article/Trump-Bump-Still Lifts/242253.

Rendon, Jim. "*Nonprofits Led by People of Color Win Less Grant Money With More Strings (Study).*" *Chronicle of Philanthropy.* May 7, 2020. https:/.www.philanthropy.com/article/Nonprofits-Led-by-People-of/248720.

Rolland, Abby. "How philanthropy and faith in diverse communities can guide us today." Lilly Family School of Philanthropy. November 13, 2018. https://blog.philanthropy.iupui.edu/2018/11/13/how-philanthropy-and-faith-in-diverse-communities-can-guide-us-today/.

Tempel, Eugene, Timothy Seiler and Dwight Burlingame, eds. *Achieving Excellence in Fundraising.* 4th ed. Hoboken, NJ: Wiley & Sons, 2016.

Singh, Devin. *Divine Currency: The Theological Power of Money in the West.* Stanford: Stanford University Press, 2018.

Saarinen, Risto. *God and the Gift: An Ecumenical Theology of Giving.* Collegeville, MN: Liturgical Press, 1989.

Smith, Christian and Hilary Davidson. *The Paradox of Generosity: Giving We Receive, Grasping We Lose.* Oxford: Oxford University Press, 2014.

Spirit and Truth. "Pandemic Perspective: Reflections from Two Church Historians." May 8, 2020. https://www.spiritandtruth.life/videos/2020/5/8/cs15aln5yd78txip87plonj69djhx7.

Teson, Katy. "*Rage Donations: Is Your NonProfit Ready for this New Trend?*" *Wired Impact* April 12, 2017. https://wiredimpact.com/blog/rage-donations-nonprofit-trend.

United Methodists of Greater New Jersey. "Weekly Survey Results from July 30,2020." https://www.gnjumc.org/covid19/resources-and-information/weekly-survey-results.

Zunz, Olivier. *Philanthropy in America: A History*. Princeton: Princeton University Press, 2012.

# PART I

When the Field Changes

# CHAPTER ONE

# Emergency Bag$ in Crisis

## *What We Carry and What We Leave Behind*

### Aimée A. Laramore

In March 2020, I was blessed to have a seat at the table when dozens of pastors and faith leaders began the navigation of the COVID-19 pandemic. As a consultant and strategist, I was humbled to be a conversation partner as ministry leaders reimagined ministry and giving during the pandemic. In this moment, listening attentively to leaders across the country, representing diverse denominations and ministry roles, the most pressing concerns had little to do with securing tithes and offerings. Instead, the priorities for virtual worship, sermon delivery, examination of congregational needs, redefined pastoral care, navigation of loss and increased neighborhood outreach dominated each and every conversation. These priorities filled each and every conversation. With the weight and demand of thousands of worshippers on their shoulders, the resounding theme was one of giving; giving more to the people who needed them during this time.

In essence, these leaders were pushing those in their ministry's orbit to leave behind the idea that the church is a building. I heard a continuing emphasis that being the church and being a Christian requires living and doing what we say we believe. As I listened to the nuanced experiences of these leaders, something didn't feel right about illuminating the best practices of fundraising. I have learned repeatedly the awkward realities of surfacing fundraising practices during times of crisis, enduring the slow walking of hard truths with those unprepared to hear feedback about weak infrastructure or insufficient accountability.

Although the pandemic was a new paradigm in these ministry conversations, crisis was not. Countless stories illuminated experiences of surviving difficult times, no matter the particularities of the challenges. There is something about the nature of crisis that makes you think deeply about what is most important. If the house is on fire, "What do you save?" Forced to think quickly and decisively about community and congregational needs, limited bandwidth and an unpredictable environment, leaders packed those things that were most essential and continued the work at hand. In difficult times, we routinely ask those that have journeyed with us before, to come with us again. Through unceasing prayers, direct service, and generous gifts people were invited to embrace opportunities to directly change lives. As fundraisers, we could have asked the question directly, "Will you be a part of the journey?"

It was apparent that people and givers were swiftly motivated to mobilize resources as the weeks progressed and community needs came into focus. An occasional joke about the importance of online giving, or drive by efforts to collect gifts and donations, did not compare to the dominant concerns of ministry to the human soul. In the midst of crisis, and the repeated illumination of racial injustice, those in my immediate circles focused their attention on the people that needed care the most. They focused on their families, staff, the elderly, church members, neighbors, protestors and yes, donors – but there was little time to worry about the ways that people would and could give to continue to support their ministry. The needs were greater than any one church or congregation.

Even in those early days, we were not operating with rose colored glasses, even as we celebrated the gift of giving. To be clear, every conversation partner recognized the potential impact of the pandemic on financial resources and bandwidth. Yet, the economic themes that filled conversations revolved around ministry to those who were unemployed or under-employed, closing the digital divide, helping individuals facing eviction, undergirding those battling healthcare disparities, addressing pervasive food deserts and efforts to identify the undeniable impact of educational inequity. At the heart of the real matters of life, new giving conversations and new stewardship practices were born. Densely layered times of crisis and injustice in our world created a laser focus on innovation and impact to meet unprecedented needs. We were leaving behind the unnecessary—complex application hoops, debilitating red tape, and decision delays.

It actually should come as no surprise, congregations rooted in generosity before the pandemic, continued to be generous in the midst of the pandemic, even with the loss of in-person worship. For six consecutive months I witnessed untold stories of generous acts, often empowering community members and lay leaders to act in courageous ways. These quiet, behind the scenes efforts, rarely garner media attention or generous praise. I can remember scrolling social media posts and noting that Alfred Street Baptist Church (ASBC) made a donation of $15,000 to Black Benefactors, an innovative giving circle dedicated to enhancing the well-being of Black children, youth, and families by encouraging philanthropy, community service, and advocacy in the Washington, DC metropolitan area. One act of innovation was captured, giving to givers.

Whenever we encounter active congregational giving, we must know that demands of mortgages, staff salaries, existing ministry, and congregant needs persist. Thus, external generosity in this way is an intentional, courageous choice. Not every congregation or donor has this capacity. For every courageous act of giving, there are deep needs in our community, and financial gulfs within our denominational brothers and sisters struggling to survive.

This season asks each of us to examine our own legacy and choices during these difficult times. There are endowment rich communities that surround us, that are resource rich, while being mission, vision and empathy poor.

I have had the pleasure of knowing Rev. Dr. Howard-John Wesley, ASBC Senior Pastor, for several years. A philanthropist in his own right, his congregation has modeled what it means to be givers for decades; the National Museum of African American History and Culture, unparalleled investments in aspiring college students, faithful service to the homeless, now, a historic giving circle. Givers give. A new orientation to stewardship means that the needs of the community will continually be synonymous with the needs of the people; and gifts directly to the community convey a belief that they are well positioned to make a difference in their own right. There are countless examples I can recount, congregations and individual donors alike, who demonstrated with their gifts an unwavering belief that now is not the time to hold more tightly to what we have. It is a time that compels more generous giving and a release of gifts to those who have demonstrated a propensity and a desire to give, steward resources and minister to human needs well.

In fundraising, we recognize that only a small percentage of our time is focused on making "the ask." We also recognize, no one solution solves the myriad of challenges that face us. The increasing efforts to create a culture of generosity illuminates the need to educate, thank, plan, evaluate, inspire, and learn as we secure resources to fulfill mission and vision. Each of us is needed, often at a level that challenges us far beyond our current comfort zone. Engulfed in the pandemic, congregations and faith communities across the nation focused on their culture of generosity, redefined. The focus on pledge seasons and capital campaigns was almost immediately replaced with efforts to *do* something that would change the quality of life of those within our sphere of influence. Crisis revealed needs for virtual worship, online Bible Study and innovation for small groups, intentional communication to every person in our midst, food deliveries and emergency funding for frontline workers, PPE needs and unplanned modifications to daily life. We are leaving behind misguided priorities.

How is it possible, absent our beloved sanctuaries, giving rituals and offering time, that many of our congregations are right now today—stable, solvent, and thriving? At its core, fundraising has always been about relationships, vision, trust and faith formation—and nothing has changed during the pandemic. Donors and generous members are realizing afresh what we've known for a very long time, that we do not live in a world of equity and justice. As images of bare grocery store shelves, downtown protests and elders in isolation dominate our screens, the ministry responses to these challenges were also illuminated and made apparent. At our best, we have been forced to over communicate our reality during this season. In an effort to communicate that we are often doing the very best that we can, imperfectly, another gift has surfaced. The poignant reminder of unmerited favor, of grace. We are leaving behind unachievable standards of perfection.

Grace shows up in consistent and faithful donors who recognize ministry must exist in different ways in order to both thrive and survive. While giving methods and systems have shifted in recent months, those positioned with technology and expertise in online giving, streaming platforms and virtual ministry initiatives have been in the best position to thrive. For others, the ministry of pen and ink has become more manageable and more meaningful as the fatigue of excessive screen time overtakes community members. While some segments of society are experiencing the differences in our communities for the first time amidst viral video clips and news stories, just as many are actively leaving behind the idea that we live in a society that aspires to be equal and just.

Whether in the protest line or sanctuary pew, passive responses no longer serve the vision of the future we want. Not everyone has experienced the same economic realities during this season. While there are indeed some industries and individuals that are thriving during this season, the impact of the pandemic on small businesses, restaurants, ministry startups, and school systems is clear.

Many of us are leaving behind the idea that we will outperform racism, outpace the fragility of our peers, or the idea that we are not at risk for being outspoken. No longer can we be simultaneously mentally sane and politically correct as a way of being. We are leaving behind the idea that we can be passive and not be part of the problem. We are leaving behind the idea that ministry is most effective in the constraints of a building with stained glass windows and neatly organized pews.

These shifts in reality and mandated adjustments to daily practice, illuminate the reality that money still follows mission and vision when needs are clear, compelling and urgent. The work of identifying needs as clear and urgent has rarely been seen as ministry, but fundraising, while too often relegated to the transactional, has the potential to fuel transformation. Obligatory giving practices have had a strong position in our faith communities and we have become accustomed to the language of what must be done to simply survive or get by. The pandemic has reminded us, in unanticipated ways that resources transform ministry and lives. We are leaving behind the notion that our gifts, financial and otherwise, can be taken for granted.

People give where they see impact and where they trust that transparency and accountability lead to their gifts being used well. As we contemplate and ponder faith and philanthropy during this season, we need not go far from the roots and foundations of our faith. Bradley Holt, author of *Thirsty for God*, states it in this way:

> People can be Christian in different ways. There are differences in beliefs, but most differences have to do with culture, ethnicity and experience. For example, some believe that Christian spirituality is best practiced by withdrawing from the world and spending the whole day in solitary prayer. Others value hard theological thinking as most important. Still others believe that working for social justice is the whole of Christian spirituality. Some feel the Spirit of God most keenly when they are witnessing to their faith to another person, others when they

are praising God in tongues, and others while receiving bread and wine in the Eucharist.[1]

In the same manner that people are Christian in different ways, people are also givers and demonstrate generosity in different ways. The wisdom and lessons learned in crisis reminds us that these differences are an inherent part of the people that support and nourish our ministry work. Donors are motivated and inspired by clear and relatable efforts to live faith and impact lives and that truth forces us to leave behind the idea that the physical church building is the essence of worship and practice. The countless efforts to preserve physical structures that have barely been used to their potential reminds us of what matters most in ministry. We are challenged to leave behind the rigid constraints of what it means to be the church. We leave behind the idea that every cause and every initiative can or should attract everyone.

The pandemic has shaped new opportunities to build and cultivate donor relationships, engaging individuals to see beyond their personal circumstances and bringing new light to alternative experiences and personal narratives. We pack lightly. Leaving behind lengthy case statements and static plans, this season has demanded fluid and decisive ways to make a difference. In the midst of unanticipated change and transition, efforts to educate, inform and update donors have been at a necessary high level. Seminaries, special programs, and churches alike are investing in elevated communication, to help donors understand their ministry work and to identify other important efforts that need help.

At our best, I have witnessed many churches and institutions focus their attention outward, to the seen and felt needs of the most vulnerable. The pandemic has forced urgency, embracing new partnerships and new levels of accountability, giving in more meaningful ways. We leave behind the belief that we are all dreaming the same American dream for each other. But people continue to give, because we do not yet leave behind hope.

1. Holt, *Thirsty for God*, 13.

2020 has reminded each of us, *carry what is most important, do good, be courageous and be well.*

## *Bibliography:*

Holt, Bradley. *Thirsty for God: A Brief History of Christian Spirituality.* 3rd ed. Minneapolis: Fortress Press, 2017.

CHAPTER TWO

# Trump, Vegan Soup, and Automobiles

## TREY WINCE

IT'S TRUE. EVEN WHEN the small-scale nonprofit leader is employed full time, it's only part time.

I vividly remember standing in the parking lot of the small Methodist church I pastored while in seminary. It was half an hour after our monthly leadership meeting, and thus, 15 minutes past my bedtime. But there I stood, attempting my best pastoral listening face as a young adult heaped piles of seething opinions on my leadership decisions—namely how much time and energy I had bothered to focus on financial sustainability and providing social event gatherings.

"I can literally go anywhere in town and have a better time than your fall festival, but I can't be pastored. I can't worship. That's what I need from this place," he said.

Admittedly, I did plenty of seething on my own, as I spent too much time over the next few days having an imaginary argument with him about the realities of our financial situation and the necessity of serious fundraising and outreach work if we were going to be able to provide him with a sufficiently-roofed sanctuary and a pastor for another 18 months.

Just about every pastor I know has had some version of this moment. This is the impossible balancing act we ask of every small church and small-scale nonprofit leader. We want them to use their time in such a way that 100% of their hours are "on mission," and we are disappointed by the creative dance that is sometimes necessary to keep the light bill paid. Meanwhile, even if they had all of the resources they needed, they would still be facing an uphill battle. By nature, nonprofit work is difficult. Nonprofit work rushes into the nooks and crannies of our world that rarely get the attention they need. Similarly, leading churches in a post-Christendom world is no walk in the park.

Once more for the folks in the back. Even when the small-scale nonprofit leader is employed full time, it's only part time.

I'll be more specific just in case you feel like you're not leading a small-scale ministry, because it's "a lot bigger than the average church in your denomination." Here goes: if your annual budget is less than $500k, I'm looking at you.

Now, before you warm up your Twitter account, hear me out. "Small-scale" is not to be confused with unimportant. Small-scale ministry is where the good stuff happens. It's where pastors make home visits, sit in the living room of a perpetually pernicious trustee member, only to finally notice that the progression of family pictures on the wall changed from four smiling faces to three some 20 years ago. Small scale is where names are known, where the real difference between Pork Roll and Taylor Ham is obvious, and where the Limbaugh-listening electrician offers a spare room to the brown-skinned lesbian who sits on the 4th row and has three weeks until her new job starts. It's the good stuff. It's . . . So. Damn. Good.

Despite these meaningful moments, small-scale ministry leaders spend a third of their time—or half if they would like Miss Clarence's Memorial Endowment to last a full decade—on developing creative ways to talk people into giving $250,000 this year so that salary, health insurance, retirement, property maintenance, utilities, the roof leak, denominational dues, the broiler, Trunk-or-Treat, and... the organist can all continue yet another trip around the sun. That's assuming the organist has it in her, of course.

We can do better.

Consider also the perennial critique of church insularity, of churches' refusal to engage in spaces that build new and unlikely relationships. And as long as we are confessing our ecclesial sins, let us also admit that the vast majority of church growth models are based on winning over the disgruntled constituency of other nearby churches.

Again, we can do better.

Meanwhile, in addition to all the familiar statistics around decreased church participation in emerging generations, we also know that President Trump's 2017 Tax Cuts and Jobs Act does no favors for the financial position of nonprofits.[1] Increased standard deductions, newly taxed fringe benefits, and an exclusion on tuition deduction will only create more pressure on the average pastor, who in turn, will need to double down on fundraising, buckle down on that annual fall retreat, and cut down the youth director's hours.

A few facts to know about our shifting financial landscape: with the 2017 tax bill, the number of people who can claim deductions has been more than cut in half, likely disincentivizing a multitude of typical givers. The Urban-Brookings Tax Policy Center estimates that this bill "reduced the federal income tax subsidy for charitable giving by one-third—for instance, from about $63 billion to roughly $42 billion in 2018."[2]

Despite all this, I have to admit that I'm pretty hopeful about a number of possibilities for this next season of nonprofit leadership. Consider one possible alternative. A lead pastor gives 20 hours to a flexible for-profit business that covers 60-70% of their annual salary. In their remaining work hours, the pastor focuses on caring for their congregants, discipling core leaders, engaging in local mission, and even the occasional sermon. Meanwhile, those 20 hours of outside work put the pastor in a new space that

1. Office of Management and Budget. 2020. Analytical Perspectives, Budget of the United States Government, Fiscal Year 2021. Washington, DC: US Government Publishing Office.

2. Urban Institute and Brookings Institution, *The Tax Policy Center Briefing Book*, 324–325.

connects them with new people outside their normal circles. Even better, the church's financial contributors will give with the confidence that comes with knowing a significant part of their money will go toward mission rather than overhead, a priority that becomes more important the younger the constituency.

Meanwhile, churches continue to want pastors who are gregarious, vision-casting, extroverts with premier communications skills. But that's not all, these pastors will also need to be organized, strategic planners who can sequence timelines, manage the budget, and coordinate a good prayer banquet. Too often, the church will end up surprised to find that they only got one of these skill sets, not both. There are plenty of analogous situations across the nonprofit world, and though this is a blunt characterization of leaders' skill sets, it does the job of pointing out that we rarely find the unicorn of a well-balanced, highly-talented leader who can wear the dozens of hats necessary in a sparsely-staffed church or nonprofit office.

Despite these realities, I see this moment in our church's history as one of significant hope. Like it or not, desperation prompts innovation, and the table is well set for both.

For the past year or so, I have had the privilege of working with Cristin Coop of Coop's Soups.[3] Cristin had a hunch that the economic model for church did not have to suck the life out of pastoral leadership. In other words, she had the audacity to believe that her church's economic model should lead to more ministry possibilities and more joy. I find this to be refreshingly different than the zero-sum tug-of-war we typically associate with mission and financial solvency. In fact, I find Cristin's entire church planting experience to lower my anxiety.

After watching her large church leadership team overextend themselves in order to sustain the church's rhythms, ministry, and income, Cristin went to Wesley Theological Seminary with a hunch that this could be done differently. She worked and saved up money while in school, and then began her church plant before graduating. Rather than take a sizable church-planting grant from

3. Cristin Coop by Trey Wince. By phone. October 28, 2020.

her United Methodist denomination (along with the accompanying benchmarks and expectations), she opted to launch a small vegan soup company out of her kitchen. Leveraging many of the lessons and rules of Zach Kerzee's Simple Church model, she committed to an income stream that:

A) Was on-brand for her ministry

B) Connected her to new people

C) Provided space for discipling others

The money she saved up during seminary provided room for a slow on-ramp as she built up her congregation and accompanying business. In just the first year, she netted $12,000 to offset her salary. This income has only continued to expand, but as important, her work has put her in meaningful relationship with countless local businesses and clients. Cristin shared: "We don't make tens of thousands of dollars yet, *but* it still takes the pressure off. We don't pass the plate, but we also have some people who quietly give. Each week, we have volunteers who help make soup with me."

Compare this gradual, trust-building church leadership process to the frenetic, pressure-laden life of a typical church planter facing grant benchmarks, denominational dues, and the waning energy of their core planting team. I think she might be on to something. Just as interesting, consider the fact that young people find Cristin's model highly compelling during a time when American Christianity's relationship with the Trump administration has done much to erode young peoples' trust in the church.

In short, Cristin has grown a church community with a transparent financial model during the hardest season in American history to do such a thing. This should grab our attention. Also, our appetites.

Denominational judicatories, despite facing a multitude of financial and participation challenges, also stand at a moment of great possibility. We would be hard-pressed to find organizations that are more asset rich than church denominations. Across our country, thousands of underutilized buildings sit staggeringly close to similar buildings of the same denomination. Being that the automobile has now been invented, and people aren't riding horseback to church anymore, I'm going to make an unpopular-but-reasonable suggestion: we don't need this many churches.

Despite the pain associated with the reality of closing and selling countless church buildings, we must recognize the spectacular possibilities associated with this moment. Denominations could once again do extraordinary things and tell a remarkable story that captures peoples' imagination for what could be. In my work with Ministry Architects and Ministry Incubators, I've sat with dozens of leaders who have clear visions for what is possible during this season. I've seen business pitches for denominations to buy for-profit prisons with the expressed goal of reversing the abysmal recidivism rates our country presently knows.[4] Judicatories could cover the costs of pastors' health insurance and retirement in a way that relieves small churches of significant financial pressure. The creative housing possibilities for financially or relationally poor folks are endless.

The bottom line is this, despite the fact that the past four years have not been good to the American church and nonprofits, this season has sparked new and creative financial models that might ultimately wake up our collective imagination. I'm feeling hopeful.

## Bibliography:

Alper, Mariel and Matthew R. Durose. *2018 Update on Prisoner Recidivism: A 9-Year Follow-up Period (2005-2014)*. US Department of Justice. May 2018. https://www.bjs.gov/content/pub/pdf/18upr9yfup0514.pdf

Office of Management and Budget. *Analytical Perspectives, Budget of the United States Government, Fiscal Year 2021*. US Government Publishing Office. 2020.

Urban Institute and Brookings Institution, *The Tax Policy Center Briefing Book*. May 2020.

4. Alper and Durose. *2018 Update on Prisoner Recidivism: A 9-Year Follow-up Period (2005-2014)*. US Department of Justice, 1–2.

CHAPTER THREE

# Faith and Philanthropy

*Moving from Mechanics to Ethics*

DAVID P. KING

AMERICAN SOCIETY IS UNDERGOING significant shifts in the ways we *form* and *fund* our life together. Research shows that patterns of philanthropic participation are changing across all types of groups and organizations, with fewer households engaging in giving, a smaller number giving much more, and many others continuing to contribute through long established religious and cultural traditions.[1] The religious landscape is changing too, with some congregations and faith-based nonprofits struggling to sustain members and budgets while others are growing. Research suggests the changes in faith and giving may be linked.[2] As religious affiliation and regular worship attendance has declined over the past decade, so have the number of households engaged in charitable giving and community engagement. At the same time, leaders in both faith and philanthropy are experimenting with new approaches to gathering, giving, and serving.

1. Philanthropy Panel Study (2001-2015).
2. Austin and King, *Giving USA Special Report: Giving to Religion.*

Both philanthropic and religious leaders are grappling, each in their own ways, with questions of money and meaning. Both groups hunger to think and talk more deeply about their fundamental purposes, in order to imagine a flourishing future for their communities. Yet the kinds of conversations that could help philanthropic and religious leaders attend to these foundational questions of purpose are not often happening, or happening well. From racial injustice, economic inequality and climate change, to COVID-19 and political polarization, questions of what it means to not only survive, but also thrive in the contemporary world are some of the most urgent of our time. The available answers and standard prescriptions have never seemed so impoverished or ineffective to so many. We need a fuller understanding of the ways in which religious and philanthropic institutions and practices have interacted to expand our imagination, making fuller sense of both traditions as well as the ways they have worked together to shape the common good. Religious communities are perhaps best equipped to speak to these questions of how we cannot only live but flourish together, yet too often these same religious communities shy away from addressing these questions directly when money is entangled with these broader themes of economic systems and philanthropic practices.

At the same time, despite its financial impact and outsized social significance, philanthropy too has often been left underexamined either as an *unquestioned good* where individuals freely give of their time, talent, and treasure or an *unwelcomed result* of political and economic systems that empower a few individuals with undue wealth and influence to shape public policy and our collective life together. With the increasing professionalization of philanthropy, public policy, and the nonprofit sector, we have tended to focus measuring the social impact on our common life through a notion of effectiveness. *The prior question, however, must be: effective at what?* In order to address when philanthropy does the public good, we must first reflect on the moral nature of philanthropy and the pluralistic visions of the public good.

What does it mean to give a good gift and how do we build meaningful relationships with one another? In order to answer this question, we need a fuller history and new voices to expand who counts as a philanthropist and what counts as a philanthropic practice. If some imagine a foundation grant or an individual donor's major gift, others would include the change dropped into a Salvation Army red kettle or the tithes placed in the offering plate. Still, others might think about the online crowdfunding for a local grassroots advocacy organization or the public-private partnership seeking to mass produce a COVID-19 vaccine. Whether described as philanthropy and charity, giving and volunteering, or even generosity and prosocial behavior, these collective practices have long played a key role in our communities on local, national, and global scales. For religious leaders, we need to bring new imagination and new tools to address the adaptive challenges their institutions are facing in working together for the common good.

As we attend to the traditions of faith and philanthropy for our current contexts today, the power of language becomes vital. Our faith traditions give us deep wells to draw from in reflecting on theological notions of charity or philanthropy, stewardship or generosity, as well as scarcity or abundance. Yet, in illustrating giving through these powerful metaphors, we can sometimes inadvertently abstract and sentimentalize faith and philanthropy removing it from any specific context. The result is often a domesticated theology that has extracted any real sense of money-talk from our faith communities individually and institutionally. In so doing, we are depriving ourselves of some of the greatest assets from within our faith traditions in order to make our case to donors and consider how best to plan for our organization's future as well as to explore new innovative practices and find opportunities to come alongside new partners for a common purpose. At the same time, relying on stewardship sentimentality and abstract money-talk also limits faith leaders in confronting issues of justice in our world where business practices, questions of privilege, and social ethics are completely wrapped up in economic issues.

These may be particularly pointed questions for us today, but they are not necessarily new. Faith communities have always faced these issues. This is what Protestant public theologian Reinhold Niebuhr saw in 1930 when he wrote a piece for the *Christian Century* entitled, "Is Stewardship Ethical?" As the story goes, the young Niebuhr had made a name for himself as a Lutheran pastor deeply engaged in social issues: pacifism, labor, and economic challenges. After just taking a post at New York City's Union Theological Seminary, and facing a deadline for submitting his regular *Christian Century* piece, Niebuhr decided to write on stewardship ethics with a fairly sweeping question: "Did the churches have anything important to say about the ethical character of the entire western civilization?"[3]

Niebuhr entitled the piece, "Is Stewardship Ethical?" as he sought to shine a light on how the church talked or didn't talk about money. It's easy for us to think that faith and finances have always been the same, but at least in the American church, what is often described as "traditional" stewardship practices and congregational finances today are a relatively recent innovation among majority, white, established, institutional churches. Only toward the end of the 19th century did denominations begin to make the case for Christians to tithe to the church out of a sense of commitment. And the language of stewardship only gained popularity between the world wars.[4] Like today, innovations in philanthropy and giving occurred against the backdrop of drastic changes in American society: widespread urbanization, immigration, and increasing tribalism. To sustain the growth of American congregations in the midst of these great transitions, denominations further developed the language and practices of stewardship. At the same time, these stewardship practices often seemed siloed from the pressing issues of the day. And so Niebuhr asked, "Is this stewardship ethical?"

Niebuhr was skeptical that conventional stewardship language could speak to current moral complexities. He called out the

---

3. Niebuhr, "Is Stewardship Ethical?" *Christian Century*, 555–557.

4. Hudnut-Beumler, *In Pursuit of the Almighty's Dollar*.

church as too easily satisfied—too quick to praise the virtue of the philanthropic gifts made by those with concentrated wealth and power. He claimed that "the apparently voluntary nature of a gift does not necessarily make it a truly ethical act." Niebuhr worried that faith and finances too easily avoided the ethical questions. How did "your man of power and privilege," Niebuhr would ask, "make his money?" How does he treat his workers? This too is a stewardship question and required what Niebuhr called a depth and range of ethical imagination. Of course, as a Christian realist, Niebuhr admitted that Protestant teachings on giving are full of mixed motives, but he challenged the Protestant churches to see stewardship as an ethical issue—personal, communal, global.[5]

Yet the churches largely ignored him. Niebuhr went on to become the most recognizable public theologian of the 20th century, and stewardship principles and techniques went on just as they had before. Scholars in their ivory towers and grass-roots advocates on the ground fought for labor, tax reform, civil rights, environmental justice, but they rarely framed this as the work of stewardship. At the same time, churches entered the most prosperous period of post-World War II institutional building and public prestige, but they rarely saw their fundraising campaigns as an ethical issue.

Perhaps, today we're in a similar time—where the issues of our day are leading us to consider the full scope of our theology, ethics, and practice. In his day, Niebuhr was responding to world wars, the rise of communism, a Great Depression, and the response of the federal government, big philanthropy, and local communities to these challenges. We too are met with evolving global ideologies, economic uncertainty and rising inequality, and a global health crisis alongside new attempts to respond from big philanthropy and traditional religious institutions. Unlike the church's response in past decades, with declining religious affiliation patterns and declining trust in religious institutions, we may not have the luxury of simply going about business as usual.

When we attend to the intersections of faith and philanthropy, it is important to remember these questions affect not only

5. Niebuhr, "Is Stewardship Ethical?" *Christian Century*, 555–557.

our institutions but also us as individuals. In reminding us of the structural questions, Martin Luther King, Jr. often preached, "Philanthropy is commendable, but it must not cause the philanthropist to overlook the circumstances of economic injustice which make philanthropy necessary."[6] At the same time, Pope Francis reminds us of the personal and relational. Preferring the language of charity over philanthropy, the pope defines the work at hand "not as a business" nor "a sedative for our restless conscience" but as "the sign and instrument of God's love for humanity and for all of creation, our common home."[7]

The intersections of faith and philanthropy are the opposite of a zero-sum game with a clear winner and loser. Contrary to popular opinion, once a gift is given, it is not simply consumed. In fact, the opposite is often the case: through the relational process of giving and receiving, there is more than what there was before, and our generosity grows through experience and community. In extending Niebuhr's question to our current context today, what would we ask? How can we embody an ethic of stewardship in our congregations that extends beyond the offering plate and funding our budgets? What is the relationship between generosity and justice? What role must our religious institutions play in rebuilding a sense of trust in our communities when working together for a shared future? How can religious leaders, out of the deep resources of our faith traditions, actively step into these vital discussions of money and meaning to shape the future of philanthropy? Moving from the mechanics to the ethics at the heart of faith and giving, we can open up our imaginations to the past, present, and future ways in which we can work for the change in ourselves and in the world that we hope to see.

## Bibliography:

Austin, Thad and David P. King. *Giving USA Special Report: Giving to Religion.* Giving USA Foundation, 2017.

6. King, "On Being a Good Neighbor," *Strength to Love*, 25.
7. Francis, "Address to Caritas Internationalis: The Meaning of Charity."

Francis, Pope. "Address to Caritas Internationalis: The Meaning of Charity." May 23, 2019. https://www.ncronline.org/news/vatican/francis-chronicles/true-charity-means-focusing-jesus-and-poor-pope-says.

Hudnut-Beumler, James. *In Pursuit of the Almighty's Dollar: A History of Money and American Protestantism*. Chapel Hill, NC: UNC Press, 2014.

King, Jr, Martin Luther. "On Being a Good Neighbor," *Strength to Love*. Boston, MA: Beacon Press, 1963.

Niebuhr, Reinhold. "Is Stewardship Ethical?" *Christian Century* 47. April 30, 1930.

Philanthropy Panel Study (2001-2015).

# PART II

## Innovation:
## The Intersection of Crisis and Care

CHAPTER FOUR

# Grandma's Table

## *Memories of Survival and Adaptation*

PATRICK B. REYES

STEAM ROSE FROM THE plate of chorizo con huevos y papas. The smells of cooked chorizo and warm homemade tortillas filled the entire kitchen. As I ripped off a piece of tortilla and grabbed a little bit of food off my plate, I savored the small bites of love my grandma cooked for the entire family.

The laughter of children and conversation between my aunts and uncles was a symphony that included the chorus of ancestors, all conducted right there in my grandma's kitchen. The burdens of hard labor, the joys of raising another generation, and the dreams of our people hung together like papel picado. Can you see the bright colors, the beauty of the scenes the paper depicts in our small home? Can you hear the music of a family's love playing? Can you feel the warmth of your ancestral cooking? Can you taste the nourishment to mind, body, and soul? Can you see the meal served lovingly on the plate, a gift from someone who loves you just because you exist? A gift freely given.

The memories of my grandma's table occupy my imagination about survival and adaptation especially in these moments of three pandemics: a global health pandemic, global planetary devastation due to the human made climate crisis, and the violence against Black, Indigenous, Latinx/a/o, and broader peoples of color worldwide. At the time of this writing, we have surpassed 9.6 million infections and 235,000 deaths due to COVID-19 in the US alone. Because of our addiction to non-regenerative energy, by 2050 scientists estimate that over 1 billion people will be displaced because of the impacts of global warming. Food and water insecurity due to climate change, which much of the world is already facing, will limit not just what my grandma could put on the table, but also what we will be able to put on the table for our grandchildren. Black and Latinos/as are subject to violence and discrimination. 2.3 million people are incarcerated in the US. 40% are Black bodies. I write in a period where those families seeking a better life and sanctuary in the United States were torn apart from their loved ones, separated in the thousands. Children locked in cages. With more than 500 children still waiting to be reunited with their families.

We did not have much, but my grandma found a way to fill our plates. My grandma's sisters, her brothers, my aunts, my uncles, my primos/as, and the generations to follow, all of our minds, bodies, and souls were all filled with her love. Her adaptation was to love every single person that crossed the threshold of her home in a world that sought to eradicate our people, erase our history, and emulsify our culture through annihilation and assimilation. She gave to us, because she wanted to see us thrive.

She gave freely. We did not demand. My grandma's table was abundance among scarcity.

For so many communities like my own, adaptation has emerged in the space between life and death. I have met death. He knows me by name. Adaptation grows from this place that the world has chosen to abandon.

My soul is troubled. I oversee and work with one of the most diverse teams in nonprofit and philanthropic spaces. We develop and distribute grants and resources to support the next generation of scholars of color and young adults who are discerning a call to ministry. I witness my field defining adaptation in ways that leave behind my grandma's table.

I am in constant conversation with a dominant culture that demands that my grandma's ancestral recipes must still privilege the continuation of the same systems of oppression that created the borderlands we occupy. Adaptation has become a definition of the privileged, to maintain dominance, status, and place in the world.

In centering my grandma's table, a table of survival, members of the privileged and dominant culture wring their hands with worry; will they be left out? My grandma's table does not exclude others. My grandma's table was a radically inclusive space. Sharing her gifts for anyone who crossed into her home passing the small altar with the Guadalupe and images of saints was her purpose and call; it is my purpose. Her table emerged from generations of surviving the pillaging, removal, and colonizing of our communities.

Adaptation comes from this survival. It does not emerge from the dominant culture's desire for the systems, rules, and structures that sought to control, rather than free. Freedom is found when I can give myself, my whole self, without demand.

Adaptation is not the dominant culture walking across the threshold of my grandma's home and demanding that they be fed, first, if possible. Adaptation is not removing her beloved from our chairs, sitting down, and declaring that they also must partake in the meal; a meal cooked for our very survival. Adaptation is not claiming the furniture, the artwork, and the ingredients as their own.

We recognize that the whole world is hungry. Hungry for more than just my grandma's cooking. The world is hungry for my grandma's love. A love that carries the heartbeat of my people for generations; a faint heartbeat that is the life drum to which our ancestors and children's children will dance.

It is a heartbeat that dominant culture has cut themselves off of through generations of pillaging and plundering. The benefactors of this pillage need repair, healing, and care. The restoration and repentance for them are not the same as the need for resurrection and ascension of our family. We are the survivors of attempted genocide against indigenous people of this land, and the remnant of a former colonial power.

In this moment, I ask myself, even in my place of perceived power, do I have the freedom to give? If I am sitting in the power of my grandma's kitchen, how do I help those adapt to survive and thrive, and not recreate structures of dominance? How do we create conditions for freedom and liberation without forgetting that my grandma's table was a place of sanctuary, a place where we could go when we had nothing? Her home was a chapel where we showed up full of hope, knowing that for just a moment we would be called beloved: for blessed are the poor.

How do we reframe liberation for the inheritors of oppression? There are those who benefited from taking from my community, who stand not just on our shoulders as we prop up the unjust and unfair system that keeps your feet on our necks, but who stand on the hallowed ground where our ancestors' and our own blood mixed with soil. How can we find freedom? How can we create a future where our children will thrive? How do we re-member the dry bones as they speak with the ground as they say to each other "we also feel this pain," because both know what it is to be drained of our sacred and divine worth?

The answers to these questions are simple. Design with the community in mind. Centering the sights, tastes, and smells of my grandma's table means we re-member the ancestors that created the conditions for us to survive. By including those in the design previously pushed to the margins, the resources draw on a well-spring of ancestral wisdom that knows how to stretch a meal, expand the table, include our neighbors, and offer respite for those who have been dispossessed.

By centering Black, Indigenous, Latinx/o/a/e, Asian and Pacific-Island peoples and descendants, the non-human, the land, and all those erased by a violent history, we recognize our work is not bound up in just this moment of time and space. The adaptation to the work is drawing far back into our ancestral lineages and memories, and casting a vision forward for future generations.

In practical terms, it means that as a foundation director, nonprofit leader, as one who sits on the boards of institutions of higher education and elementary schools, as a partner, father, friend, as a Chicano, as a person of faith, I sit between generations. I am the bridge between the five generations back, to the first Carmelita I have a record of carrying that name. I sit between my grandma Carmen, my daughter Carmelita, and the Carmelita (or spirit of her) that will emerge in five generations to come. I am an ancestor in training. Adaptation is honoring those generations of survival while building the world I want that young woman in five generations to inherit.

Adaptation defined by my grandma's table begins with us who have been left out. It asks, "What do you want, mijo and mija?" It listens deeply to that answer. It means that the spirit of love will be carried into the domain of faith-based nonprofit, ecclesial settings, and philanthropy. Those who know how to adapt were already on the margins before the triple-pandemic, eating at my grandma's table.

We should listen to my grandma's wisdom.

For those in dominant culture, adaptation means learning to sit and wait in my grandma's house for food. You will eat. Trust you will be taken care of and you will be loved. Your adaptation will be learning to see that we can all eat. There will be no more privileging dominant culture as center. You will be part of our sacred practices of unlearning your violent histories, healing from the pain you and your ancestors caused, and sitting with our stories of survival. You will need the humility to adapt to this new reality where you do not have more, where you will have to be patient, where you will have to think about harmony with the world and others, before and over self.

For those at my grandma's table, adaptation means stepping into your power in this moment. You are the teachers. You are the powerbrokers. We have a chance to design with our healing in mind. We have the opportunity to design the worlds our children will inhabit. Let it be like our grandma's table, not a reflection of the dominant culture's world that necessitated its existence.

May we build a world of abundant love for lives here and there and those yet to come.

# CHAPTER FIVE

# Collaborative Partnership

## *Christian Ministry in a post-Pandemic World*

### THAD AUSTIN

OVER THE LAST SIX years, I have studied innovative Christian leaders who are pursuing congregational social entrepreneurship. Congregational social entrepreneurship is a form of philanthropic ministry connecting a congregation with its community by engaging the free market and, at times, generating income. Among others, you might think of congregational social enterprises as coffee shops, thrift stores, bookstores, restaurants, co-working spaces, and even hotels.

Although congregational social entrepreneurship may not be the calling of every Christian leader or the right form of ministry for every congregation, I have observed an attribute among congregational social entrepreneurs that is universally applicable. Collaboration is required. I believe that these forms of partnership will be increasingly necessary for Christian ministry in a post-pandemic world.

## The Collaborative Partnership

Charlene is the pastor of a diverse and growing evangelical congregation in the Southwestern United States. Her congregation opened an off-site restaurant and catering business employing at-risk young adults. In addition to its everyday operations, the social enterprise provides after school programs, life coaching, and opportunities for discipleship.

I sat with Charlene at one of the restaurant's dining room tables just before the after school rush. When I asked her about the origin of her social enterprise, she began describing the team of lay and clergy leaders who each drew upon their unique backgrounds, skill sets, and expertise. She said, "We are collaborative in how we come up with new projects." The team dreamed, planned, and launched the ministry together.

As I interviewed other congregational social entrepreneurs across the United States, I heard this story repeated again and again. Regardless of geographic region, denominational affiliation, theological tradition, racial or ethnic composition, size of budget, or number of members, congregational social entrepreneurs are collaborative. In my research, I found no evidence of a congregational social enterprise that was able to launch or sustain operations without a partnership between lay and clergy leaders present.

## The collaborative partnership is one of the "social" aspects of social entrepreneurship

One clergyperson I interviewed described the relationship by drawing a distinction between an architect and an archaeologist. While an architect can draft plans alone in an office, an archaeologist works with a team. As buy-in is gained from lay and clergy leaders, congregational social entrepreneurs develop coalitions of supporters and volunteers.

A collaborative partnership draws on the complementary gifts of laity and clergy. Those with commercial experience bring their understanding of business to bear on the form and structure of the social enterprise. Clergy draw upon their theological understanding to support and preserve the social enterprise as forms of ministry. When this partnership forms, clergy develop a greater appreciation for the gifts and experiences of laity, and laity deepen their understanding of ministry and their appreciation for their pastor.

## When leaders rely on one another, a bond begins to form

I met with Kevin, a lay leader of a large, affluent, mainline congregation in the Southeastern United States. One of the most successful businessmen in his community, Kevin provided financial capital and business acumen to help support his congregation's social enterprise—a coffee roasting company. When I met with Kevin, he described the relationship he developed with his pastor when establishing the business:

> I was moved by what they set out to do [in the social enterprise] based on our pastor . . . with whom I had a very special relationship. . . . That project and just our rapport was a real bonding opportunity for [us]. . . .

Kevin went on to describe the uniqueness of the relationship he shared with his pastor, as different than he had ever experienced with any other clergyperson he had ever known. Together, they discovered how their individual vocations could come together to support the congregation they loved. As their partnership solidified, both men began to develop a deeper appreciation for the calling of the other. When a collaborative partnership forms, trust and mutual respect develops between leaders.

## The collaborative partnership provides strength in times of need

Opposition to a congregational social entrepreneurship can be fierce. Some congregational leaders report losing up to thirty percent of their membership when they launch a social venture. Many are concerned about the "church is becoming a business." The partnership between lay and clergy leaders provides wherewithal to face these and many other challenges.

I spoke with Randy, the pastor of a small charismatic congregation in Pacific Northwest. His congregation converted the church's historic parlor into a coffee house open to the public throughout the week, even on Sundays. Randy described the coffee house as one of the most effective platforms for ministry he had encountered during his long career. In the early days, however, the idea felt risky.

Randy was concerned not only with the fallout of converting one of the congregation's historic spaces into a place of business, but also the long-term consequences if the venture failed. If the coffee house floundered, he worried how members of the congregation would react the next time he introduced an innovative idea.

I asked Randy what gave him the determination he needed to move forward. He responded, "I had confidence in my leadership and my board. They would not . . . walk away from me." The collaborative partnership provides confidence that congregational leaders will be supported in times of opposition and be able to draw upon each other's strengths in times of need.

## Why are collaborative partnerships important?

Collaboration increases the willingness of lay and clergy leaders to innovate, take risks, and get beyond the church's walls. Partnerships give energy for productivity and incubate creative ideas. However, the reason that collaborative partnerships matter is not simply because they make us more effective or efficient.

Collaboration is important because it makes us more faithful. Partnerships provide opportunity for communal discernment and direction (see Prov 11:4; 15:22). Together, leaders debate, refine, endorse, and adopt a shared vision. As one clergy leader said:

> [D]eep prayerful risk that is discerned by a community, and not by a singular person, is often the way . . . I believe entrepreneurship breaks through because it's born in the heart of God and not in the heart of the person with a great idea. . . . None of this happens without [the community].

Collaboration changes not only how we act, but also who we are. It expands how we think, feel, and understand our context. It introduces new ideas and brings us together.

## Partnerships reflect what it means to be the body of Christ and the people of God

The biblical narrative reminds us that we need each other. As Paul writes, "The eye cannot say to the hand, 'I don't need you!'" (1 Cor 12:21, NIV). Think about some of the partnerships described in Scripture: Moses and Aaron, Rahab and Joshua, Ruth and Naomi, David and Jonathan, Mary and Martha, or Paul and Barnabus. Which of these leaders could say that their partner was unnecessary?

We cannot do the work of ministry alone. Collaboration gives us a glimpse of who God is: Father, Son, and Holy Spirit. When we collaborate with others in work that is prayerful, holy, and selfless we may begin to understand something of the mysterious and wonderful trinitarian partnership. Perhaps this is one of the reasons that Jesus sent the disciples out two by two and prayed that they might be one (Luke 10; John 17).

Prior to the global pandemic, American congregations faced many headwinds: declining worship attendance, increasing religious disaffiliation, and tighter church finances just to name a few. The pandemic has also introduced an additional impediment that is even more insidious. If left unchecked, it will certainly exacerbate these trends. Namely, many of us have learned to live, work, and even pray alone.

## As a result of COVID-19, we have become increasingly comfortable with distance

Stores mark the floor to keep customers six feet apart. Plexiglass separates cashiers from the checkout line. Masks hide our faces. During the pandemic, these measures saved lives, kept our economy afloat, and served as demonstrations of solidarity and loving concern.

If we are not careful, however, these cultural practices may begin to subtly suggest that we are better off apart. Like the religious leaders in the parable of the Good Samaritan (Luke 10), we may become comfortable simply passing by on the other side.

Ministry in a post COVID-19 world needs to bring people together, and partnerships are one of the most effective ways I have seen for that to happen. Leadership, responsibility, and ownership must be extended beyond a single individual. Collaboration serves as an outlet for guidance, encouragement, and mutual support. This is what Martin Luther called, "the priesthood of all believers."

While providing opportunity for innovation and new forms of outreach, COVID-19 has also increased the uncertainty many congregational leaders feel with regard to the future of American religion. I have found that collaborative partnerships are both necessary for the development of a congregational social enterprise and critical for its success. However, this type of leadership is not limited to a singular form of ministry.

As the church enters a post-pandemic world, collaboration is required.[1]

---

1. This chapter has been adapted from the forthcoming book *Congregational Social Entrepreneurship: A Field Guide for Lay and Clergy Leaders* by Thad S. Austin, scheduled for release in 2021 by Wesley's Foundery Books, GBHEM Publishing.

CHAPTER SIX

# Bricks and Mortals

*Sacred Space and the Faithfulness of Letting Go*

EMILY HULL MCGEE

ONCE THE SITE OF ecclesial innovation for the sake of the city, the cavernous gym at First Baptist Church on Fifth filled up that day with relics of ministry years gone by and bargain-hunters picking through the spoils.

That gym was the first of its kind in downtown Winston-Salem, North Carolina, built sturdy and central for 1950s-era outreach when the church house of a southern city really was a hub of its communal life. For decades, community Friday roller-skating nights and youth basketball tournaments, pot-luck suppers and preschool activities brought thousands of local citizens into our space, these guests often transitioning into church members (and tithers!). Many of these good folks grew in their discipleship and their sense of belonging to God and one another, and from that entry point, formed the solid foundation of First Baptist on Fifth's institutional support and allowed the church to thrive by every modern-era metric.

Decades later, Planet Fitness and the like had pulled community members from our fitness space into their brighter, shinier, newer ones. Better social options for Friday nights filtered out a regular stream of visitors, and the landscape of downtown Winston-Salem swung several times as industry moved out and innovation moved in. As the years passed and as people's rhythms and preferences shifted, membership in our traditionally-oriented, historically-rooted congregation fell. Spaces once filled with people were now clogged with... well... *stuff,* the detritus of decades of ministry now spread around the gym floor.

The auctioneer's tinny voice echoed around the cinderblock walls, glancing off our collection of treasures now caught — not by moth or rust — but obsolescence. *There they were — the former things.*

"Do not remember the former things," the prophet Isaiah cries out to the people of Israel (NKJV, Isa 43:18). But didn't Isaiah know that these are the people of memory? They remember the covenant the Lord made with Abraham; they remember what the Lord did when they were enslaved by Pharaoh in Egypt; they remember the long road to freedom through sea and shore; they remember the taste of liberation that put manna on their lips; they remember the wilderness that tried to rob them of their lives; they remember the years of wandering, yearning to find their way and find themselves. And now, exiled in Babylon, they remember Zion, they remember what had been. *Don't remember the former things?,* I imagine them to say. *The former things are what got us here! They're central to who we are!*

This kind of "former things" identity crisis that Isaiah names sounds familiar to me and the remarkable congregation I pastor. For years, our people watched the three buildings that constituted our church house become ever more complicated to manage. In those 112,000 square feet, it seemed there was always something going on with the building! If it wasn't the leaky roof that caused peeling plaster on the chapel walls, it was the leaky roof that caused peeling plaster in the Sanctuary, or the stairwell, or the organ chamber, or the choir room. If it wasn't the original plumbing that caused backups in the kitchen sink, it was water that got in through the windows in the education building. If it wasn't a failed or aging HVAC unit, it was the constant thrum of the state regulators who always ended their annual inspection of our 5-day, 5-star, community-beloved children's childcare center with the ominous warning, "you know, someday, this building is not going to be grandfathered in anymore..."

These concerns mounted, as they do. And as much as we might have wanted to ignore it, the crises in our sacred space were unavoidable. In particular, I remember a patriarch who shared some real talk at a church business meeting when confronting all that was hard: "I think we oughtta forget about it. And if it comes up again, we oughtta forget about it again!"

Perhaps worse than any broken system or leaky roof, we realized this pattern of misallocated energies on our facilities was stripping the church of hopeful energies for ministry. What spaces once prioritized innovation had become the same spaces causing deprivation. What dollars once were spent proudly to build had become the dollars spent anxiously to keep. What long memories once defined the church at its flourishing had become the blind spots blocking a vision for what new thing God might do in our midst. Without a change, the former things would become the final things.

So, a committee began the research. A year later, another committee did the work. Rather than sites of stalemate or agenda-pushing, these committees became spaces of honesty and holy discernment. God's Spirit so firmly occupied these spaces with us, breathing unity and possibility where each of us had once held fast to doubt or despair. And after months of conversation, prayer, and tears, we looked the former things squarely in the face. We gave thanks for what these former things had been and done, praised God for the work of love to which they had born witness, and released them from our grip. For us, that meant a renewed decision to stay put, to root ourselves firmly in our downtown home, and double down on one of our deepest commitments of place in the church's nearly 150-year history. But in order to stay there, it also meant pruning away, with great sadness, that which we could no longer sustain: tearing down two of our three underutilized and costly buildings (that held the aforementioned gym, the chapel, the fellowship hall, and dozens of Sunday School rooms), emptying ourselves of their contents, shrinking our physical plant by 67%, closing that beloved Children's Center, and entering an arduous and complex $6M capital campaign and building project to restore, enable, and secure one building to stand on its own.

The grief of losing beloved spaces and signature ministries was significant enough, but the ever-present layer beneath was that of identity. *Who would we be if not the church with the gym or the Children's Center?*, we questioned. *How will we fellowship without a Fellowship Hall or study without Sunday School rooms? What will our city, our neighbors, our friends think of us when they find out that the First Baptist Church, once flush with resources and status and power and influence, now has to downsize simply to stay alive? What if we never grow again to the size and the scope we once were? If we let go of our space, ordinary bricks and mortar that have enabled extraordinary encounters with God, what will we have to let go of next?*

Time and time again, when we found ourselves caught in the grip of an identity crisis, God's enlivening Spirit beckoned us relentlessly to hear the ancient promise echoing throughout time and space: *I am about to do a new thing; now it springs forth, do you not perceive it?*

Eight months into the coronavirus pandemic, these lessons rise fresh and raw. The irony is not lost on me that the very week in mid-March that we paid the final bill to our contractor, completing this years-long journey on our space and ready to claim it anew, became the week we shut the doors and shifted nearly every aspect of our church's life away from our physical home. Like so many around the world, we have surely grieved the losses this season has wrought upon and among our beloved community: saints in our midst, rhythms that ground and renew, structures that give meaning and life, confidence in what is unfailing and true, and the sacred space we've fought to rediscover.

And yet, I can say that we are in a healthier, more honest and fiercely hopeful place than perhaps ever before. Somehow, our muscles of upending it all, changing everything we know, rethinking church from the ground up, and unburdening the church of tomorrow from the accounting of yesterday, are muscles we have gotten used to exercising. We have learned again the faithfulness of letting go. Our journey with our facilities has taught us the vastness of God's presence, bold and boundless in its scope, is undeterred by our efforts to hold fast to these nostalgic former things. *For I am about to do a new thing,* we hear the Lord speak into this chaos, this disorientation, this detritus of ministry as we've known it to be. It sounds of hope undimmed by despair, light persistent in every darkness, love where all find a home. It sounds of a God whose abundance has the holy face of a dark and empty tomb.

*Now it springs forth, do you not perceive it?*

As the story goes, a pilgrim was walking along a road when one day he passed what seemed to be a monk sitting in a field. Nearby men were working on a stone building.

> "You look like a monk," the pilgrim said.
> "I am that," said the monk.
> "Who is that working on the abbey?"
> "My monks," said the man, "I'm the abbot."
> "It's good to see a monastery going up," said the pilgrim.
> "They're tearing it down," said the abbot.
> "Whatever for?" asked the pilgrim.
> The abbot paused with a knowing smile.
> "So we can see the sunrise at dawn."[1]

---

1. With gratitude to my friend, Rev. Dr. Paul Baxley, who shared this story in a sermon at First Baptist on Fifth on April 8, 2018, encouraging us in our work. It is attributed to Johannes Tauler, German mystic and contemporary of Meister Eckhart.

# PART III

## From Barriers to Opportunities

# CHAPTER SEVEN

# The Generosity of Death

## KEVIN KIM WRIGHT

In Min Jin Lee's masterful novel, *Pachinko*, she traces the multigenerational trek of an exiled Korean family fighting desperately for a future that never seems to materialize. Sunja, the humble matriarch, wrestles with her relationship with Hansu, a Korean businessman whose child she bore when she was a teenager. As the two grow older, Sunja keeps Hansu at a distance until one day he gains an audience with her after revealing that he is dying. As the two sit and discuss Sunja's family and seemingly stable life, Hansu strikes up this conversation:

> "Are you okay living here?"
> She nodded.
> "And the little boy. He's well behaved."
> "Mozasu checks in on him all the time."
> "When will he be home?"
> "Soon, I better make dinner."
> "Can I help you cook?" Hansu pretended to take off his suit jacket.
> Sunja laughed.
> "At last, I thought you'd forgotten how to smile."
> They both looked away.
> "Are you dying?" she asked.

"It's prostate cancer. I have very good doctors. I don't
think I'll die of this. Not very soon, anyway."
"You lied then."
"No, Sunja. We're all dying."[1]

Christians are no stranger to death and yet, when given the
chance, we take every opportunity to avoid it. Even Jesus denies
death the satisfaction of taking his friend Lazarus away in John
11. What does it say that the Word Made Flesh, cannot even bear
to see his friend come to an end? Why, like Sunja, do we tiptoe
timidly around the inevitability of death? Perhaps it is because humans are embodied creatures, bound to creation both emotionally
and elementally. We are doing our best to eke out every last minute
of existence we can because this world, as God described it in the
beginning, is *very good*.

At some point, however, the fear of losing everything we've
worked towards becomes a crusade against the natural passing of
time. We will not live forever. The things we build will not infinitely
endure. Time will march on and we will at some point fail to keep
pace with its forward momentum. This is the fear of almost every
congregation I've ever encountered. For some, the anxiety mani-
fests itself with how long they can maintain the organ, upkeep the
stained glass windows, or operate a physical space built to hold the
crowds of Christendom at its peak. For others, the fear presents
itself as a panic about losing the church's youth to a secular world
and seeing the next generation of Christ-followers sink into the
morass of moral relativism.

Ironically, the way congregations choose to address both of
these fears is often the same: raise more money. Money to pull off
a successful capital campaign and endow the maintenance of the
organ till kingdom come. Money to hire a young adult minister
or start a "contemporary worship service" that packs more people
into the pews (or rows of chairs, most likely). Money to renovate
the youth room and build a cavernous "family life center" to ensure
young people never stray far from the church. Money becomes the
mechanism by which we stave off the anxiety resulting from our

1. Lee, *Pachinko*, 352–353.

impermanent existence thus making the avenues and customs by which we raise those dollars as sacred as Moses' meeting with God on Mt. Sinai.

For many congregations across America, a pledge campaign, or variation thereof, is the primary bulwark for supporting a church's fiscal health. Churches painstakingly produce a "Steward-ship Sunday" or obsessively curate a series of worship designed to help people make a decision to invest in God's work manifest through their local congregation. Carefully crafted testimonials, slickly edited videos, and glossy pledge cards are mere table stakes when it comes to playing this game.

The need to pull off these elaborate campaigns has even given rise to an entire market of literature and professionals ready to help congregations dig up the dollars necessary to add on an education wing, repave the parking lot, or simply meet the needs of the an-nual budget. These "giving guides" or "generosity consultants" help ensure that congregations need not worry about having to one day turn off the lights for the last time. Maybe *some of you* are dying, but please don't assume anything about *our* fate.

What happens then when a catastrophic event upends the tactics churches depend upon in order to fight for their futures? What happens when churches can't gather at full strength each Sunday and when people must maintain social distance from each other? What do we do when the handbook provided to us by our "generosity consultant" doesn't have a chapter on dealing with fun-draising during a global pandemic? How do we stave off the death of our institutions when the best tools for preservation that we had at our disposal seem ill equipped to confront the unprecedented challenges we face?

When COVID-19 struck, the organization where I work faced a difficult decision. Due to pandemic protocols, we cancelled our primary fundraising event: a large gala charged with raising critical dollars that allowed us to provide educational opportuni-ties for under-resourced youth. Without our primary fundraising event of the year, we faced the terrible reality of deep staff cuts and a drastic reduction in services. For years we relied on a fairly standard approach adopted by many nonprofits in order to keep things going and without that avenue available, we were running into a dead end.

Our gala provided us with an opportunity to bring people together into one space and dazzle them with the stories of our students' success. Operating on the scripted stage of a banquet hall, we could present a carefully packaged presentation showcasing the work we do through stunning student speeches and tightly scripted presentations. Losing the ability to physically connect with donors undermined our organization's efforts to connect with donors in an intimate and meaningful way.

The stalemate over what to do was finally solved by some of our gifted teaching artists who had been impressively holding virtual classes over digital connectivity tools like Zoom and Discord. Their success at connecting with students across social distance made us contemplate using those platforms to provide a way for us to tell our story to donors. However, as anyone who has ever participated on a Zoom call or Google Hangout knows, anything can happen when we begin to open up parts of our lives not previously visible to others. Our students live in small apartments, have unreliable internet connections, and contend against a choir of sirens, barking dogs, and noisy family members in the background. If we wanted to communicate with our donors and have them hear firsthand from the students we serve, it meant fully accepting the aspects of life we were accustomed to editing out, the parts we deem largely unacceptable to others.

The Jesuit priest Fr. Greg Boyle touches on this idea in his book, *Tattoos on the Heart*. In his chapter on Compassion he retells the story of "Loony," a 15 year old gang member who was recently released from juvenile detention. As Fr. Greg and Looney sit in his office, the young man becomes emotional as he expresses his strong desire to just "have a life." Fr. Greg uses his experience with Looney to reflect on Jesus's strategy with people who often felt wholly unacceptable to the world. Fr. Greg writes, "He (Jesus) eats with them . . . He goes where love has not yet arrived, and he 'gets his grub on.' Recognizing that we are wholly acceptable is God's own truth for us — waiting to be discovered."[2]

Over the past few months, my organization has discovered our "wholly acceptable-ness" by giving up on any highly polished fundraising campaigns. Instead, we invite donors to visit our virtual classrooms where students forget to mute their mics and our teachers compete with singing *abuelas* and younger siblings watching cartoons too loudly in the background. We've had an internet connection cut out leaving a student's face frozen in time right as she was sharing about her future hopes (a better internet connection is one of those hopes, no doubt), and we've overheard someone's uncle discussing a minor medical issue that we all pray has been resolved by now (for both his sake, and ours). We are unabashed that this is our work and that these are the families we are so honored to serve. We invite guests to become a part of this very human community for which a glossy brochure or a news-room quality testimonial cannot do justice. More times than not, this approach has led to our community becoming larger, not smaller.

Perhaps poetically, this shift into digital space has grounded us in a more powerful physical reality. Take away the fancy sound system, three course dinner, and guests of honor, and what you are left with is an authentic understanding of our mission as it lives on the ground amidst students and their families. Accepting the death of the old way of doing things and braving the invitation to connect at the raw edges of existence has given us a more profound understanding of life together and deepened our commitment to a common mission.

Despite our best efforts, so many of the in-person and physical tactics we deploy to raise funds often do the exact opposite of what they are intended to do. Rather than cultivating intimacy, community, and solidarity among us, our efforts to encourage generosity all too often create distance between us and our neighbors. We are accustomed to placing before our pledgers the very best parts of our work and the aspects that we hope stir souls and call forth compassion. And yet, what better way is there to achieve

2. Boyle, *Tattoos on The Heart*, 71.

those goals than by grounding ourselves in "everyday existence" and adopting a truly incarnational approach to philanthropy in which everything we bring—barking dogs and all—is acceptable to God? What if we spent more time looking for the choicest offerings among the ordinary and often overlooked? There is no greater call to generosity than the Word Made Flesh who went on a righteous rampage to redeem and reclaim everything about our humanity, including the unsightly parts.

A few years ago, I was leading a class on Christian approaches to social justice and decided to have one lesson focused on examining the life of Dorothy Day. At the end of the discussion, an elderly woman named Margaret piped up and said, "I actually met Dorothy Day." The class' attention turned to Margaret who went on to say, "Well, actually it was more of a run-in." As it turns out, many decades before Margaret was a student studying social work in New York City. One day her class went on a tour of the Catholic Worker offices. As the students were listening to a social worker talk about the organization's services, Dorothy Day bustled out of an office and charged right through the group of students, oblivious to their presence and obviously overwhelmed with the myriad of issues competing for her attention. As Dorothy stepped into an open elevator, Margaret recalls that the veteran social activist shook her head and mumbled, "I need to get out of here or this place will be the death of me."

Day's aggravated comments on what was no doubt a frustrating day at work are as prophetic as they are profound. Sometimes remaining in the same place is the most dangerous thing to do. Are we so cemented to fundraising structures and strategies that have outlived their effectiveness that we are willing to risk actually accelerating organizational and institutional decline? Or, do we have the courage to look honestly at ourselves and recognize that sometimes letting things die is the only way to truly live?

If we were to answer the latter question in the affirmative, we would find ourselves asking an entirely new set of questions when it comes to thinking about expressions of giving. What would a pledge campaign look like if it were to focus more on inviting others into a beautifully unscripted and completely unpredictable common life together rather than simply replaying a highlight reel over and over until people finally open up their checkbooks or Venmo app? What if we approached helping others become more generous with their money by first inviting people to become more generous and welcoming of all aspects of their humanity and the humanity of their neighbor? What if we allowed ourselves to not rely so much on the industrial complex of development consultants and instead relaxed our fears of what may come in the future (as if we had any control over it anyway)?

There will understandably be great sadness and even fear when confronting the death of things upon which we have long relied. We might be tempted to deny the changing of circumstances and press forward with a playbook that was not written for the time in which we find ourselves. But the danger here is that if we refuse to look for signs of death, we will be unable to decipher the signaling of imminent resurrection. As the women on Easter morning discovered, to meet the newness of God you must leave behind the comforts of home and head straight for where you know death to dwell.

Perhaps the greatest gift of changing the types of questions we ask ourselves is that over time we will become less obsessed with institutional survival and more concerned with modeling faithful Christian practices that cultivate virtuous living. We become less concerned with dying and more joyful about living fully into our abundant existence as people of God. The Christ who opened up his life to us provides us with a model of how to open our lives up to others, including the parts we typically put on "mute." Radical love such as this has the power to awaken a holy, fearless, and uncoerced generosity rejoicing in the goodness of this world and the world to come.

## Bibliography:

Boyle, Greg. *Tattoos on The Heart*. New York: Free Press, 2010.
Lee, Min Jin. *Pachinko*. New York: Grand Central, 2017.

# CHAPTER EIGHT

# Reimagining Church Buildings

*From Liability to Asset*

## Dave Harder

I GREW UP IN a home where hospitality was deeply valued. We always had guests around our table, often from other cities and countries. As a young boy I recall sitting with friends and family around the dinner table captivated by the stories. I grew up in a small rural town with little exposure to other places; going to the city to shop was a big deal! However, our table was the exception to the limited exposure rule. We had people visiting from other cultures and contexts. Their stories taught me that not everything was like my own experience of a small, rural setting. Over time, these stories became a form of grounding, locating me in a larger narrative, expanding my perspective of what it means to be human in the world.

Each of us come from narratives and stories that form and shape our particular way of being in the world. Within a community or institution, shared experiences and stories can also become collective assumptions, boundaries, ways of believing that create a sense of security and comfort and direct how we fit into our greater context. What happens when our dominant stories and narratives are challenged?

We are living in an unprecedented time. In this moment the places I serve are becoming increasingly aware of systemic problems like income inequality, insufficient elder care, food insecurity, racism. All of this while experiencing collective mental trauma, financial strain, and political polarization. These cumulative factors lead to anxiety as we face an uncertain future. While the coronavirus pandemic has exposed and amplified these problems, they are not new. I suggest we are in the midst of a massive cultural shift. The way we have accepted the world to be is no longer. We are not going back to "normal." Our pre-corona existence was not normal; rather, it normalized greed, inequity, exhaustion, extraction, disconnection, racism, and scarcity. We should not long to return.

We've been given the opportunity to create a new narrative.

As someone who works primarily with mainline congregations, I hear a familiar story; it revolves around declining (and aging) attendance, long-overdue maintenance, lack of missional imagination, and stretched budgets. As I sit with congregational leaders, I am dumbfounded, given the larger narrative of decline, the resistance to engage in honest and critical assessment.

Recently, I had a conversation that reflected this reality. I was sitting with one pastor and he said, "Dave, I am one 90-year-old away from dying from a crisis." My response was "Sir, I think you have been in a crisis for a long time."

The challenge I see with our faith institutions is the desire (and sometimes, expectation) to stay the same in an ever-changing context. I am often invited to consult in order to discover a path forward, but very quickly I find that few are interested in changing. *What they really want are creative ways to stay the same.*

My consulting work takes me to musty church basement meetings with committee members. I was in one of those meetings talking about how this beautiful sanctuary that sat 500 could be a multi-purpose space for the community. That would mean getting rid of the pews, something I quickly learned was a sore spot for many. One of my more interesting moments was when a parishioner took me by the hand and led me into the sanctuary to convince me that the pews were comfortable. She believed so deeply that pews were sacred that she could not see the ways in which they were a hindrance to community and space. They were *not* comfortable.

The congregations that I have worked with love asking what I call "Church Questions." What about the pews? The liturgy? Can we keep the choir? Do we have to change our style of music? In asking these questions members assume that everyone wants the same kind of church that they want. But what if we looked around and noticed, not who is here, but who isn't here, and then got curious enough to ask the "why" questions.

Churches and clients get stuck in a story, in a narrative, in the way things are, and measure their success according to that narrative. In working with congregations the same series of questions emerge:

- How do we get more young people?

- How do we grow Sundays?

- How do we increase committee involvement?

- How do we add to the choir?

- How do we increase our budget?

All these questions are part of a dominant script that we have come to believe about what it is to be the church. The script that says church is what happens in the building for a few hours on a Sunday and that our success is dependent on that one event. We must interrogate the narrative and let a new one emerge. One that places less emphasis on the success of a Sunday and more on the hopes and dreams of God for the neighborhood. For many congregations this work can start with them bridging the dreams of God of the neighborhood with their buildings. Moving the conversation from Sunday to everyday and church buildings from liability to asset.

As a church family, many of us have inherited valuable real estate from previous generations. Our facilities have served admirably, hosting weddings and funerals, baptisms, worship services, and music concerts. They have also served the community through Scouts, AA, daycares, fundraising dinners, and so much more. Unfortunately, these buildings often become millstones around the neck of congregations as energy is diverted from mission into roof repairs, work parties for painting, with declining, precious funds sent off for ever-increasing utility bills.

As churches struggle with these new realities, then add no rental income and the challenges of gathering that has been accelerated in many cases by COVID-19, they invariably turn to the possibility of sale. In my context alone we are expected to lose 30% of our church buildings over the next 5 years.[1]

I often hear two stories. One is the sale of the land for highest and best use, padding the pockets of an already dying congregation just to prolong the inevitable. The other is continuing on with what they have, trying to make the best of a bad situation. Neither story is compelling; one ignores the social capital these churches have been for decades in the community and the other is a slow dying to the possibility of what could be if they joined together with the dreams of God for their place.

I also see a problem within cities of isolation, loss of third spaces and few opportunities for intergenerational connection. When infused with a vision for missional presence, churches can become places of belonging that provide a natural fit for a range of social-purpose partnerships (i.e., community hubs, affordable housing, the arts). While hundreds of churches have explored opportunities to leverage their land for broader social purposes, very few have been successful.

What I have experienced in this work is an overall excitement around the "possibility" of change but then reality quickly sets in, or should I say fear takes over. I get it; change is hard! Members have lived into a narrative of church being a certain way for so long while neglecting to consider what new or next could look like. Then add the realities of aging members, volunteer drain, overall weariness, and building fatigue. As I sit and reflect on why so many congregations have started the journey with excitement and then

1. Natalie, "A Hope And Prayer For Places of Faith."

for some reason fizzled out, a catalogue of reasons comes to mind. For some it was the financial burden, for others they acted too slowly, for others they made the decision to go back to who they were, and for others it was governance models or the leadership of a few that stifled the momentum. If I was to choose one reason, it is fear. Fear of the future, fear of change, fear of losing the past, fear of moving forward into the unknown.

Stories have power to form imagination. It is hard to picture something new existing outside of the stories we hear, of what others have done. Stories spark imagination and possibility. They also ground and root us in a localized story of place and people. When transformative stories are told place, they attend to place, linking people together across place.

In a context where there are so few stories of innovation, what if we had stories that reflect a new imagination for our buildings, and leverages the asset of real estate for sustainable mission in the neighborhood? I believe there is a way forward that links our buildings and assets to the stories of the people and the dreams of God in our neighborhoods.

In my work with Parish Properties we provide a hybrid approach that avoids selling the asset while at the same time leverages development to provide the necessary capital to pay for the upgrade of the space and enhance the mission of the church. We understand there is not a one size fits all plan. Some communities of faith are property rich and cash poor. They face dwindling attendance, shrinking cash reserves and spiraling expenses. Others recognize that, while financially healthy, their property isn't stewarded to its full potential. Others are experiencing developers gentrifying their neighborhood and wonder how the parish can/should respond. In each scenario, our goal is to provide a solution that allows the congregation to clarify its missional objectives, animate its presence in the neighborhood while leveraging their land asset for mission.

We measure our success against what we call the quadruple bottom line: concern for the environment, spiritual health, financial sustainability of the congregation, and social impact in the neighborhood. Each dimension would have different objectives centering around these four principles. For example, respecting and restoring landmark assets, lowering your environmental footprint, creating a sustainability showpiece, improving neighborhood connectivity, awakening spiritually to God's mission in the neighborhood and (almost invariably) being financially successful.

So where do we begin? When it comes to our buildings and the burden they carry, how do we move from fear and loss, knowing that not acting will result in sale, to abundance and innovation? Here lies the inherent problem, *the real crisis we face is a lack of imagination*. The first step in getting to that place where we can imagine again is interrogating the dominant cultural narratives of success, our relationship to money, fear and scarcity, individualism, and polarization. The world has changed, how we gather has shifted, the last question on my neighbors' mind on a Saturday evening is where to go to church on Sunday morning. As we engage in asking the hard questions of why we do what we do and are curious with the thoughts and dreams of our neighbors this first step invites us to imagine what the church could be in our context, here, now, in this place and time.

In this cultural moment, where what it means to be the church is shifting, it has given us the opportunity to reflect on multiple narratives that we previously just accepted. Narratives of colonialism, systemic racism, financial inequality, and environmental issues. Confronting these narratives will help challenge our beliefs about what's possible and connect our view of land and buildings to a much larger story. To have a healthy social fabric we need healthy community spaces. Spaces to "bump" into one another and foster connection. When we restore a degraded or unanimated space we restore our connections to each other and to our community. To shift our imagination and challenge our beliefs about church space we will need to ask questions like:

- What is the history of our building?
- Who has been left out or not included?
- Who is our property and building for?

- What are the cracks and crevices in our community?

- What are the dreams of our neighbors?

- How could our building be an intersection of community and connection in our neighborhood?

Our questions matter and so does our context and place. We will not come to the solutions we need from prescriptive models given to us from the latest book or conference alone. We must move beyond a prescriptive model and begin to look and listen to the people around us; listening to our neighborhoods and communities. It is nearly impossible to love our neighbors if we don't know our neighbors. And herein lies the tension of our times; *we live in such a connected world with such limited connections.* Could we imagine the answers that will propel us into a vibrant and flourishing future are not going to be found inside a church building but on the sidewalks, in coffee shops, and on front porches in our neighborhoods. Could we be brave enough to move beyond the security of our old narratives and begin listening to the stories that are bubbling up from our place.

I would add one last thought to this conversation: *this moment requires urgency.* Engaging with neighbors takes time, figuring out property development plans takes time, getting sign-off from multiple layers of bureaucracy takes time. COVID-19 appears to have both expedited the urgency (budget holes, less rentals, less collections), and given a further excuse for inaction and navel gazing (can't really do anything now...). Inaction in this moment is actually saying something. As I meet with congregations, I sense they are waiting for all this to pass and they will experience the vitality and growth of years past. Sadly, in moments of crisis, waiting just acknowledges the path of death we are on, a hospice care of sorts, a sense of holding on peacefully until we pass. I am taken with the words of novelist Arundhati Roy:

> Whatever it is, coronavirus has made the mighty kneel and brought the world to a halt like nothing else could. Our minds are still racing back and forth, longing for a return to "normality", trying to stitch our future to our

past and refusing to acknowledge the rupture. But the rupture exists. And in the midst of this terrible despair, it offers us a chance to rethink the doomsday machine we have built for ourselves. Nothing could be worse than a return to normality.

Historically, pandemics have forced humans to break with the past and imagine their world anew. This one is no different. It is a portal, a gateway between one world and the next.

We can choose to walk through it, dragging the carcasses of our prejudice and hatred, our avarice, our data banks and dead ideas, our dead rivers and smoky skies behind us. Or we can walk through lightly, with little luggage, ready to imagine another world. And ready to fight for it.[2]

We have been given, in this moment, a chance to rethink and reimagine. Take a moment to pause and envision our buildings as places where we find joy, beauty, connection, and cooperation, a space where we weave a fabric of love and care in the world, starting with our neighborhood. The path for that new story to emerge is in taking action now. What would it look like to interrogate the narrative while being curious enough to listen? How can congregations, begin asking "now what?" In exploring and experimenting there is opportunity for creating new stories of hope and inspiration in a shifting world. Through holy imagination, our listenings can turn our buildings from liability to assets.

*Bibliography:*

Roy, Arundhati. "The pandemic is a portal." *Financial Times.* April 3, 2020. https://www.ft.com/content/10d8f5e8-74eb-11ea-95fe-fcd274e920ca.

Natalie, Bull. 'A hope and prayer for places of faith.' *National Trust Canada.* April 22, 2016. https://nationaltrustcanada.ca/online-stories/a-hope-and-a-prayer-for-places-of-faith.

2. Roy, "The pandemic is a portal."

# CHAPTER NINE

# Seeing our Rooted Good

## *Trees, Pandemics, and Economic Imagination*

SHANNON HOPKINS AND MARK SAMPSON

THE FABRIC OF SOCIETY in the US has been fundamentally tested in 2020 in extraordinary ways. Greg Jones, Dean of Duke Divinity School, refers to the four pandemics of 2020: COVID-19, systemic racism, economic disruption, and mental health distress.

This complex web of pandemics is extraordinarily challenging for many communities. We suggest that in these painful and liminal moments, there is the quiet offer to renew our imagination, particularly at the nexus of faith, philanthropy and institutions. In the midst of the challenges of meeting urgent needs, changing patterns of work and supporting vulnerable congregations, it can easily get lost that the most important question is not "What do we do next?" Instead, we suggest the defining question is always "What do we *see*?"

We contend that these four pandemics, in very different ways, bring to the foreground a certain fault-line in our modern social imagination, a fault-line that shapes what and how we see.

F.S. Michaels argues that our culture is enthralled by a "master story," which quietly influences us as individuals and as a society.

This master story is primarily drawn from mainstream economics, with these "economic beliefs, values and assumptions... shaping how we think, feel and act."[1]

The root of this economic master story is a particular conception of what it means to be human. Mainstream economics posits that the human actor is a rational, self-interested individual, who, when given a choice, will always choose that which brings happiness (utility) and avoids pain. These series of assumptions enable the science of economics to make predictions, build models and increasingly influence every area of society and culture, including the design and management of institutions.

Theologians, along with practically every discipline in the humanities and social sciences (as well as a number of Nobel prize winning economists), have long critiqued these assumptions as problematic and even destructive.[2]

At one level, it is easy to critique the reductionist assumptions of mainstream economics, particularly when comparing them to a theological anthropology. However, we contend that the economic master story primarily impacts the world not by rationally persuading us of these claims but primarily by shaping our imagination.

James K. A. Smith, in his Cultural Liturgies series, explores how participation in our marketized culture and society form us through the liturgical shape of economic practices.[3] These liturgies shape our desires and imagination. As theologian Kathryn Tanner suggests, this shapes us to the extent that, "Our ability to imagine alternative economic structures is constricted and constrained."[4]

1. Michaels, *Monoculture*, 9.

2. For a recent theological critique of capitalism, see Tanner, *Christianity and the New Spirit of Capitalism*. Also, see Poole, *Capitalism Toxic Assumptions*. David Brooks, in *The Social Animal*, creatively surveys the last thirty years of social scientific research, offering a very different picture of human nature to *homo economicus*. Many recent Nobel prize winning economists have also critiqued certain assumptions of mainstream economic theory—Elinor Olstrom, Richard Thaler, and Robert Shiller being key examples.

3. Smith, *Desiring the Kingdom*.

4. Tanner, *Economy of Grace*, 33.

What does this master story mean for faith, philanthropy, and institutions?

The challenge is that when we survey the landscape of faith, philanthropy and institutions we are conditioned by the "master story" of economics to *see* disconnected individual institutions and organizations in competition with each other for scarce resources. Institutions and organizations concerned in a moment of complexity and chaos, above all else, for their own survival. Organizations that are unintentional echoes of the anthropology of economics.

We imagine a disconnected and competitive landscape, and so that is what we inhabit.

An example will help illustrate this. A philanthropic institution wants to tackle a systemic problem in a particular city. It follows the well-trodden path of an open, competitive grant program. Through the different efforts of individual nonprofits, the institution hopes to learn more about what programs "work," so it can scale solutions in other cities.

What are the assumptions that are made with this approach? Firstly, systemic change takes place primarily through the actions of individual nonprofits. It is organizations that are the locus of transformation. Secondly, that competition between organizations for a scarce resource is the condition that creates creative and efficient programs. Assumptions that echo our modern economic master story.

Of course, crucially, this is not the only narrative that is being played out in leadership teams, grant committees, and board meetings. It is not all that we see; it does not determine everything we do. If the master story of economics is the map, it is important to remember that "the map is not the territory."[5] However, it is our cultural default setting and we need to be attentive to its ability to shape our imagination, particularly in moments of crisis. Maps matter.

In order to move away from this master story, we need a new paradigm with a new language of connectedness.

5. Korzybski, *Science and Sanity*, 58.

Where can we look for resources for a paradigm shift towards a new imagination?

We could be inspired by the rebirth of trinitarian theology in Western Christianity, where the doctrine of the trinity moved from being a rarely addressed endnote in systematic theology to being the starting point and the key to unlock much recent profound theological insight. This paradigm shift has helped create a new language and theo-logic of relatedness, mutuality, and interdependence.

We could look at the paradigm shift in physics—the dramatic shift from Newtonian physics to quantum physics. As physicist Nils Bohr famously said, "Those who are not shocked when they first come across quantum theory cannot possibly have understood it."[6] At one level, this was a shift from seeing individual "things," such as atoms, as the basic building blocks of reality, to seeing the significance of the *relationships between things* as the core fabric of reality.

Trinitarian theology? Quantum Physics? Or, we could just look at trees.

Our understanding of trees has fundamentally shifted in the last 25 years. Previously, we understood trees through a modern (perhaps even economic) lens. Individual trees compete with other trees for the resources they need: predominantly water, sunlight, and nutrients from the soil. As such, the trees that grow faster and have larger canopies dominate their environment. It is a race of individual trees for the scarce resources in their natural environment. (Enter Darwin from stage right). The strong survive.

Then, along came Suzanne Simard, a Canadian forest scientist, who, following a hunch derived from a lab result, designed what would turn out to be a revolutionary experiment.[7] In the forests of Northern British Columbia, she injected one radioactive carbon gas into a bag covering a Paper Birch tree. She then injected a different kind of radioactive carbon gas into a bag covering a Douglas Fir tree. An hour later, she discovered that both trees had

6. Heisenberg, *Physics and Beyond*, 206.

7. Simard, *Finding the Mother Tree*.

traces of the carbon from the other tree. Remarkably, it turned out that the trees were passing carbon between each other. A slew of experiments were then conducted. When the birch was leafless and the fir tree was growing, the birch would send more carbon to the fir than it received. Correspondingly, if one of the trees was predominately in shade, it would receive more carbon from the other species. These trees—different species—weren't just talking to each other, they were interdependent—communicating with carbon, nitrogen, water, phosphorus, defense signals, and more.

The idea of individual trees being in competition with each other began to unravel.

The key to understanding this communication between the trees is that there are huge numbers of fungal roots that connect the different trees in a forest. This creates a web, humorously nicknamed the *world wood web* by forest scientists. Forests are networks. An example: within these networks are hub trees (sometimes called mother trees). Hub trees are older, larger trees, who send nitrogen, carbon and phosphorus through their roots, through the mycelian web to young growing trees. They even reduce their own roots to make space for the growing young trees. Remarkably, when hub trees begin to die they push nutrients down into the mycelian network to support the young trees.

Peter Wolleben, author of the remarkable *The Hidden Life of Trees*, summarizes a key insight:

> When trees grow together, nutrients and water can be optimally divided among them all so that each tree can grow into the best tree it can be. If you "help" individual trees by getting rid of their supposed competition, the remaining trees are bereft. They send messages out to their neighbors in vain, because nothing remains but stumps. Every tree now muddles along on its own, giving rise to great differences in productivity. Some individuals photosynthesize like mad until sugar positively bubbles along their trunk. As a result, they are fit and grow better, but they aren't particularly long-lived. This is because *a tree can be only as strong as the forest that surrounds it.*[8]

8. Wolleben, *The Hidden Life of Trees*, 16-17.

The older, modern paradigm meant we saw the resiliency and productivity of an individual tree as factors solely influenced by what that individual tree can acquire from its surroundings. This new and emerging paradigm tells a very different story: resiliency and productivity are not characteristics of an individual tree but rather characteristics of the forest. It is the *connections between* trees that matter most.

Does this paradigm shift in forest science offer hope for our weary institutional imagination?

How might we learn to see networks and not just individual organizations, to see collaboration as an essential characteristic of flourishing, to see interdependence as a quality of resiliency and not a weakness? How might institutions see "their" resources as both something received from a network and also as a gift to that network?

So, returning to our starting question, when we look out on the landscape of faith, philanthropy and innovation, what do we see? With renewed sight, we can see green shoots of hope all around. One example is the concept of Network Leadership, which explores the role that institutions can play in shaping networks through four principles: humility, not brand; trust, not control; mission, not organization, and node, not hub.[9] This concept is developed through two remarkable case studies: Habitat for Humanity Egypt and Guide Dogs for Blind Association in the UK. Two institutions embodying a "forest imagination."

So imagine with us. Grant programs that design for collaboration throughout the entire process. Institutions that intentionally resource their "competitors." Executive Directors reporting to their board about their contribution to other organizations. A renewed attentiveness to the connections between us, that combine to form our rooted good.

9. Wei-Skillern and Marciano, "The Networked Nonprofit."

## Bibliography:

Brooks. David. *The Social Animal: The Hidden Source of Love, Character, and Achievement*. New York: Random House, 2011.

Heisenberg, Werner. *Physics and Beyond: Encounters and Conversations*. New York: Harper & Rowe, 1971.

Korzybski, Alfred. *Science and Sanity: An Introduction to Non-Aristotelian Systems and General Semantic*. Laxeville, CT: International Non-Aristotelian Library, 1958.

Michaels, F.S. *Monoculture: How One Story is Changing Everything*. Canada: Red Clover, 2011.

Poole, Eve. *Capitalism Toxic Assumptions: Redefining Next Generation Economics*. London: Bloomsbury, 2015.

Simard, Suzanne. *Finding the Mother Tree: Discovering How the Forest is Wired for Intelligence and Healing*. New York: Knopf Doubleday, 2021.

Smith, James K. A. *Desiring the Kingdom: Worship, Worldview, and Cultural Formation*. Grand Rapids: Baker Academic, 2009.

Tanner, Kathryn. *Christianity and the New Spirit of Capitalism*. New Haven: Yale University Press, 2019.

————. *Economy of Grace*. Philadelphia: Fortress Press, 2005.

Wei-Skillern, Jane and Sonia Marciano. "The Networked Nonprofit." *Stanford Social Innovation Review* (Spring 2008): https://ssir.org/articles/entry/the_networked_nonprofit.

Wolleben, Peter. *The Hidden Life of Trees: What They Feel, How They Communicate—Discoveries from A Secret World*. Vancouver: Greystone, 2016.

# PART IV

Crisis and Care Embodied

# CHAPTER TEN

# Philanthropic Redlining
## Working Twice as Hard for Half as Much

### ERIN WEBER-JOHNSON

SOME MOMENTS CHANGE YOUR life. In 2015 Project Resource was created as a collaborative initiative between the College of Bishops, Development Office of the Episcopal Church, and the Episcopal Church Foundation to train diocesan teams from across the Episcopal Church on effective fundraising strategies rooted in a deep theology of giving. I was asked to serve on a faculty team and provide training in year-round stewardship and major gifts.

At the inaugural event, late 2015, I stood in Denver, in front of 12 Episcopal bishops and their diocesan teams. My job, during that session, was to provide national data on generational characteristics and teach how to apply this data to implement corresponding fundraising strategies. After years of teaching and preaching to congregations and judicatories, my goal was to provide relevant data to resource all congregations in my denomination.

I failed.

At the end of the segment, Bishop Eugene Sutton noted that while the national data seemed to reflect those in his diocese in predominantly white parishes, it did not reflect what he knew of parishes with majority people of color. He asked if there was such data available for the creation of additional strategies. At that time I was completely ignorant to the fact that the national data did not reflect congregations of color. I asked others in the room if they were aware of the information that Bishop Sutton needed and was met with additional requests.

So, I promised Bishop Sutton to locate this information.

After a year of asking every denominational body and every major religious research entity, I came to the painful conclusion that the data not only didn't exist, but it didn't exist for a reason. Comments from colleagues and conversation partners expressed a tacit desire, but an unwillingness to fill this gap: "We've always wanted that data." or "When you get it, we'd be happy to use it." Or "Our congregations (presuming white) need helpful strategies in engaging a broader (BIPOC) set of donors."

I also encountered lackluster institutional motivation to engage in this work, specifically to benefit and resource communities of color. Without a team created that was dedicated to provide research for the use of fundraising strategies specifically for communities of color, this problem would either not be addressed or would not be created to support the communities of color that participated. Ultimately, white folks, like me, would continue to teach and utilize strategies based on dominant/white data at all levels of our institutions. When unexamined, dominant/white data becomes embedded in institutional funding structures and evaluation matrices, only continuing the racist and inequitable models.

In the years that followed, a team of renegade leaders were brought together by the Holy Spirit, drawn together by an imagination of what was possible and a passion for this project. We founded a nonprofit, The Collective Foundation, and raised funds from across denominations in order to ensure this research would take place. I went into this work (and some might argue remained) consistently blind to the institutional barriers. My blindness to these barriers often remained until running straight into them at full speed. The Collective Foundation, filled with far more brilliant minds than my own, often navigated the institutional realities of politics and power while carefully checking my implicit bias as a white woman.[1]

We found that data talks.

It is difficult to overstate the importance that data plays in the world of nonprofits who often live and die by their ability to hit benchmarks. Charity Navigator and similar nonprofit rating organizations have dramatically reshaped the philanthropic land-scape by focusing on the numbers. In addition to giving records, churches submit yearly reports to judicatories which often deter-mine both their ability to receive various levels of support and the ability to apply for denominational specific grants. But, data on its own can't extend care and numbers on their own can't tell the whole story.

Throughout this work, as I considered my role as a former grants officer turned fundraising consultant, I was struck at how many ways well intentioned data is used in ways that limit or discriminate against Black, Indigenous, People of Color (BIPOC) leaders and the nonprofits they represent. As one might expect, my nonprofit studies as a graduate student emphasized the centrality of measurement and evaluation. I was deeply formed to under-stand that we need the right data, and right data still needs to be deployed effectively. In my work specifically around fundraising and stewardship, I have always turned toward the data. Instead of relying on "tried and true" methods, I sought to ask "What is the data saying about the moment in stewardship" and, from the answers, creating "sustainable" plans for the communities I served. Data and measurement have shaped my vocation.

But, what happens if the data is flawed? What do we do when the numbers have been manipulated? What happens when we've been asking the wrong questions? What happens when we are schooled to ask inadequate questions? What happens when the data becomes weaponized? What happens when it becomes

1. With gratitude to The Collective Foundation Founders and Board: The Rev. Larissa Kwong Abazia, Aimee Laramore, The Rev. Dr. Derrick McQueen, The Rev. Mieke Vandersall and our analyst, Dr. Amy Thayer. https://collectivefdtn.org/.

yet another brick in a solid and expanding series of walls between communities of color and access to the resources and promises of a supposedly free society?

What does it mean when data is used to inhibit BIPOC and their ministries from receiving resources?

These boundaries and barriers are often associated with redlining. Redlining itself refers to the intentional practice begun in the Great Depression era of the 1930s when government policy intentionally segregated housing stock, creating access to homes for white middle and working class families while largely pushing people of color into urban housing projects. Using red ink, lenders outlined on paper maps the parts of a city that were considered at high risk of default, as well as more desirable neighborhoods for approving a loan. Neighborhoods considered risky were predominantly Black and Latinx.

Black families lost out on at least $212,000 in personal wealth over the last 40 years because their home was redlined.[2] However, the impact of redlining goes beyond the individual families who were denied loans based on the racial composition of their neighborhoods. Many neighborhoods that were labeled "Yellow" or "Red" by the Home Owners Loan Corporation back in the 1930s are still underdeveloped and underserved compared to nearby "Green" and "Blue" neighborhoods with largely white populations. Blocks in these neighborhoods tend to be empty or lined with vacant buildings. They often lack basic services, like banking or healthcare, and have fewer job opportunities and transportation options.[3]

In short, redlining is economically enforced segregation.[4] While initially this phrase was located in conversations around real estate, redlining occurs across institutions and has taken several forms with the resulting impact continuing to be the hoarding of resources by those in power. While the practice has been in play

2. Brooks, "Redlining's legacy: maps are gone, but the problem hasn't disappeared," para 4–5.

3. Lockwood, "The History of Redlining," para 2–8.

4. Stone, "A Hard Look at Philanthropic Redlining," para 2–3.

for generations, it has only been within the past few years that the term "philanthropic redlining" has been widely utilized when talking about the difficulties BIPOC encounter when either leading or fundraising for nonprofits, churches, and academic institutions.[5] This term, characterized by how systems of power and wealth distribute resources disproportionately, developed and deepened as stories of systematic racism within granting and fundraising have been shared and examined.

In my own work and vocation I've witnessed, and at various times unintentionally contributed to, this type of redlining in my roles in the church.

A few years ago a client of mine attended a judicatory meeting where regional churches were gathered to discuss their budget. A concern was raised about continuing to support churches, specifically churches of color, that were utilizing allocated funds from the judicatory's budget. Two churches were held up as an example: one primarily consisted of Latino/as, and the other members were mostly Vietnamese and Lao. The church with primarily Vietnamese and Lao constituents was historically noted to have used judicatory funds to support the mission of their congregation but "successfully moved to a place of sustainability." Given this example, the leadership of the judiciary determined that the Latinx/o/a/e congregation should surely replicate their experience and determined their continued funding would be based on their ability to meet these benchmarks of sustainability.

What went unmentioned was that a significant proportion of those in the Latinx/o/a/e faith community were undocumented and migrant workers. Never mind that in a time of significant fear around immigration and our federal government, congregation members hesitated signing pledge cards or making financial promises. If one congregation could make the benchmarks, then why not another? Judicatory support for their mission became contingent upon this congregation working above and beyond their circumstances, culture, and counterparts. Further insulting,

5. Rendon, "Nonprofits Led by People of Color Win Less Grant Money With More Strings," para 6–8.

to ensure this congregation didn't become too dependent, funding to the Latinx/o/a/e congregation from the judicatory would taper each year by half.

As a colleague shared, they were expected to "work twice as hard and for half as much."

In the past few years, as the term philanthropic redlining became more readily known, studies have examined how money has been distributed and to what end. A fellowship program designed to provide influential leaders with resources for deepening their engagement in the world, Echoing Green, recently investigated their own granting practices. Echoing Green released results in May of 2020 after analysts examined three years of funding data. Analysts found that white-led groups had budgets that were 24 percent larger than those led by people of color. It also found that groups led by black women received less money than those led by black men or white women.[6]

Not surprisingly, in addition to receiving less, groups led by BIPOC were asked to perform significantly and measurably more in order to receive funding.[7] For nonprofits that focus on some similar issues, the gaps were even larger. Among groups focused on improving life outcomes of black men, revenue at organizations with black leaders is 45% lower than groups led by people who are white.[8]

Our systems are developed and maintained in ways that continue to mean BIPOC work twice as hard for less resources than their white counterparts. The absence of data in giving is but one way in which this has occurred. White folks, like me, utilize national data to provide best practices, reinforcing a dominant narrative. Thus, our stewardship resources in the church are created in a way that ensures white resources stay in white institutions.

6. Rendon, "Nonprofits Led by People of Color Win Less Grant Money With More Strings," para 6–8.

7. Rendon, "Nonprofits Led by People of Color Win Less Grant Money With More Strings," para 6–8.

8. Dorsey, Bradack, and Kim, "Racial Equity and Philanthropy: Disparities in Funding in Funding of Leaders of Color leaves Impact on the Table," para 2–10.

I see the irony in producing data to describe how granting organizations and major donors aren't funding BIPOC at the same levels, with varying rules around approval, and all with an absence of giving data. We need new data, but we also need something more; we need new eyes to see the racialized reality of our institutionalized funding structures. We need new questions to consider who and what does and doesn't "count" in decisions about funding. We need new ways of imagining our common life.

Darrell Hammond, Founder of KaBoom! recently noted: "Being brutally honest, my drive towards data, dashboards, and measurement—because 'data don't lie'—was wrong, especially if you're not asking the right questions, drawing the wrong consultations or insights, or not understanding the nuance of the numbers."[9] The data, or absence of it, reflects the breakdown of trust as does our own understanding of what it means in relationship with one another.

Wetikos is an Algonquin word for a cannibalistic spirit that is driven by greed, excess, and selfish consumption (in Ojibwa it is windigo, wintiko in Powhatan).[10] Interestingly, in this tradition, the spirit deludes its host into believing that cannibalizing the life-force of others is a logical and morally upright way to live.[11] This holds true for cultures and systems; all can be described as being wetiko if they routinely manifest these traits. This spirit has often been described to explain the impact of the white man on nature when enslaving people of color.

As a white person, I wonder about the impact of the commodification of bodies and the ways it has led to colonized-framed measurements of efficiency, success and profitability. Is the consequence that we continue to see resources given to "good investments" while utilizing misinformed and prejudicial data? What does it mean to have to persuade others that you/your organization

9. Foxworth and Bugg-Levine, "How to Avoid Excuses That Prevent Grant Makers From Aiding Black-Led Organizations."

10. Levy, *Dispelling Wetiko: Breaking the Curse of Evil*, 21.

11. With thanks to Alvin Zamudio for the formation and reference.

is a good investment? That your dignity, as a child of God, is worth giving to?

Within the spirit of Wetikos, how have dominant systems devoured the resources of others and, in the process, seen the erosion of life from our churches? The erosion from our own souls?

Ford Foundation President Darren Walker recently noted, "As funders, we need to reject the impulse to put grantmaking rather than change making at the center of our worldview." Walker describes how listening, learning, and lifting up voices who are most proximate and most essential to unlocking solutions is critical to the type of change making that we seek. This requires examining what gets in the way of trust—including deeply rooted cultural norms and structures, including racial biases.[12]

For the Collective Foundation, who as I write this is finalizing the analysis due in Spring of 2021, we learned that the work was so much more than the data. Relationships formed with and by our team, and with those participants involved in the study, were transforming. I can no longer teach, consult, or write without giving witness to this reality. As I make sense of systems with this newly named lens of philanthropic redlining, I try to liberate my imaginations from the spirit of Weitikos—which threatens to devour us all. Together, we work for systems where no one has to work twice as hard to get half as much.

### Bibliography:

Brooks, Kristopher. "Redlining's legacy: The maps are gone, but the problem hasn't disappeared." *CBS News.* (June 12, 2020), https://www.cbsnews.com/news/redlining-what-is-history-mike-bloomberg-comments.

Daniels, Alex. "Ford Shifts Grant Making to Focus Entirely on Inequality." *Chronicle of Philanthropy.* (June 11, 2015), https://www.philanthropy.com/article/ford-shifts-grant-making-to-focus-entirely-on-inequality.

Dorsey, Cheryl, Jeffrey Bradach and Peter Kim. "Racial Equity and Philanthropy: Disparities in Funding for Leaders of Color Leave Impact on the Table."

12. Daniels, Alex "Ford Shifts Grant Making to Focus Entirely on Inequality," 2–8.

The Bridgespan Group (May 4, 2020), https://www.bridgespan.org/insights/library/philanthropy/disparities-nonprofit-funding-for-leaders-of-color.

Foxworth, Rodney and Antony Bugg-Levine. "How to avoid excuses that prevent grant makers from aiding black led organizations." *Chronicle of Philanthropy.* (June 29, 2020), https://www.philanthropy.com/article/how-to-avoid-excuses-that-prevent-grant-makers-from-aiding-black-led-organizations.

Koenig Stone, Henry. "A Hard Look at Philanthropic Redlining." Unbound Journal Online. (February 23, 2019), https://justiceunbound.org/philanthropic-redlining/.

Levy, Paul. *Dispelling Wetiko: Breaking the Curse of Evil.* Berkeley: North Atlantic, 2013.

Lockwood, Beatrice. "The History of Redlining." Thought Co. (June 16, 2020), https://www.thoughtco.com/redlining-definition-4157858.

Rendon, Jim. "Nonprofits Led by People of Color Win Less Grant Money with More Strings." *The Chronicle of Philanthropy.* (May 7, 2020), https://www.philanthropy.com/article/nonprofits-led-by-people-of-color-win-less-grant-money-with-more-strings-study/.

# CHAPTER ELEVEN

# St. Lydia's

## *How One Faith Community Transformed Their Money Narrative*

MIEKE VANDERSALL

I SAT ACROSS A dinner table with a group of young adults in a small storefront in Brooklyn, NY. The ceiling was filled with twinkle lights and hanging ornaments, as we were in the middle of Advent. A pot of homemade soup was on the stove and hot tea was given to me upon my arrival. Generosity, in the form of hospitality, met me at the door as we were there to talk about our relationship with money.

St. Lydia's Dinner Church was my client, and this small new church met over dinner to share the meal each week. We were meeting this night, myself as their fundraising consultant, their Pastor, Emily Scott, and the fundraising committee, to explore our money stories. From these stories we sought to free ourselves from the baggage and shame we held so tightly. This freedom would allow us to move into asking others to be part of this community by supporting it financially.

The majority of congregants around the table were from the Millennial generation. Many of them were trying to figure out how to be an adult, while living anxiously on low salaries and high New York City rent. Their first real memories of money revolved around the stock market crash in 2008. Stories of evangelical-leaning congregations that pulled funding from missionaries and charity-driven programming. Stories of realizations that adults handled money, and children didn't. Stories of fear that now that they are becoming adults themselves, they are worse off than their parents, and that they, in fact, don't know how to accrue, let alone manage, money. Finally came knowledge that here they are, a new church, with responsibilities that they had never had before, and weren't sure they wanted.

Throughout my career I have found myself walking alongside congregations and leaders, helping them ask questions and solve problems that might seem insurmountable. In the liberal, white Christian church, the place that I know best and from which I come, quandaries around money seems to hold a whole lot of weight. At times money can feel like an albatross around a congregation's neck. There are those that feel guilty about the wealth they have accrued through systems of white supremacy, there are those that have a building and with it a legacy to maintain that they don't know what to do with, and there are those that just wish we didn't have to talk about money, or raise it. I often find the disconnection between money and spirituality, let alone money and what the Bible has to say about it, to be profound. It is fascinating how we seem to distance ourselves from our wealth, as it so often represents shame and confusion, albeit most times unconsciously.

God created the heavens and the earth, and it was declared good and we were to care for it and to share it. But pretty quickly we started inserting our own tricky ways of organizing things. The debt economy was put in place with due haste and over and over again there were attempts to recalibrate our pernicious efforts to ignore our shared frailty. Through the gathering of tithes. And Jubilee.

Biblical stories cast a vision for an alternative economy, and provide practices that are a consistent reminder that we are creatures created to be good, yes, but also interdependent, and also frail. In the act of engaging in these practices, in gathering our money and possessions that actually belong to God, we are provided opportunities to transform ourselves.

It is this transformation that I seek for myself and my clients, as I walk alongside God's people, asking questions, helping to solve problems.

At some point, several years into my consulting work, and several years into the life of St. Lydia's Dinner Church, I was asked to come in and help. It is hard to start a church from yeast and flour. They needed some water to mix in.

St. Lydia's is a Lutheran congregation, and it had received significant national and regional church funding to kick start its ministry; but these funds were drying up. As I listened and learned, I realized there were many money stories at play in this little congregation: the judicatory's money story, the congregants' money stories, and the pastor's money story.

Judicatory money is critical for new churches of all denominations. It's given with a great deal of excitement for what might come to be, but it is also given in all instances I have seen with a set of expectations. Some of these expectations spoken—that congregation will be formed and soon able to pay all their own bills—and some of them inferred—that the money has somehow purchased loyalty, undying appreciation, gratefulness at the expense of difficult conversations, and in many cases, acceptance of abusive treatment from governing bodies and their officers. I have found an underlying belief that the money belongs to the judicatory, not to God, and not to the wider community.

At St. Lydia's, there was the colliding of the money story of the judicatory, along with the story of the congregants, and of course the story of the pastor, for whom when we first started working together had raised a significant amount of money herself for this ministry. It is, however, really hard to raise money for a thing that you start yourself, and she needed accompaniment in this journey. To be honest, she also, unintentionally, like countless other church planters, was systemically put in positions of subservience to the institutions she desperately needed help to just to add water to turn yeast and flour into bread. In each case, these stories expressed an institutionalized money story of the church itself, the larger church, that places positive value on being self-sustaining, for congregations to pay their own bills based on their congregant's giving, and through the accumulation of wealth through the years.

As I educate myself more on how money, possessions and accrued wealth is approached biblically, I find a wider and wider gap between the things I read in the Bible—about the joyful accumulation and redistribution of resources, and regular lectures and case studies via parables from Jesus on how holding on to wealth is an effort to control our own lives that doesn't work and distracts us from our love of God—and the ways that we use money as charity with strings attached, as a way to control, manipulate, and silence.

Ecclesial innovation takes place in the site of rupture between our inherited money stories and the alternative economy Scripture outlines.

That is hard, though, for church plants, like St. Lydia's, especially made of young white folks of a generation most often worse off than their parents, who are trying to make it in a big city that they can't afford. It is hard for church plants who do not have what white, established churches often have in cities—buildings to rent, endowments, legacy gifts when long-time members die. Now, I know that churches with these things have their own set of problems, and their own story of money. Believe me I know this. But what I have found in this congregation is a practical need for dependency on higher judicatories who presume the definition of success as enough people, and enough people who hold wealth in particular, to reach self-sufficiency.

*The problem is that, again, biblically speaking, going it alone is not a thing. It is not a goal, and it simply does not work.*

Many years ago, when I was first asked to consult with St. Lydia's, we worked on expanding the circle of folks for whom the congregation was critically important beyond regular congregants to those who might not attend but found meaning and purpose in the community of St. Lydia's. We gathered all across the country, in small groups and at parties. We made our case, and we asked. We were successful. This was paired with the exploration of money stories referred to at the beginning of this chapter. Barely considering themselves adults, it was quite a leap to think concretely about paying all their own bills for the congregation.

Fast forward, and like many other churches, St. Lydia's experienced a series of transitions. After the founder left, an interim pastor stepped in, followed by an installed pastor.

The installed pastor told the congregation that cultivating donors who were not regular attendees was not an acceptable way to fund the church. During this time, to be honest, there were moments of questioning how, and if, they would continue.

After the relationship was dissolved with the former installed pastor, a new interim pastor, Christian, was appointed. I was one of his first "getting to know you" calls he made. We began talking about the money story of this congregation. He came to work with St. Lydia's with a huge heart, a ridiculous gift for words, a belief in what God is doing in this congregation, a distinct ability to heal deep wounds created over the last several years, and an appreciation for the toxic shame that continued to linger around the congregation's money story. Christian understood they needed a different path.

He was convinced that the money story of this congregation could be rewritten, and that in doing so we would rewrite our own individual money stories. He crunched the numbers, he made graphs, and in this he cast a vision: if monthly recurring gifts doubled, St. Lydia's would be able to be free from financial support from the judicatories. This is a very steep goal, but it is one that is attainable. I was hired back to help organize and frame our work together for the fall of 2020.

In the midst of a global health pandemic and in an election year, we set out to reach the goal. But first we needed to take some time set apart to examine how we got to where we are. We held an online retreat first where we gave voice to the money story of the congregation. Stories of hurt and hope were shared. Biblical stories were interpreted and reinterpreted. Money, possessions, assets, they began to shift as a source of power and control over us in our minds, into a source of collective, communal power for good. We began to see the money and possessions we owned not as a reflection of our goodness and our worthiness, but as a way that we could make a real difference in the world together. We then engaged in exercises of asking. Calling people up, having real conversations about money, its role in our lives individually and corporately. Turns out asking, while exposing our vulnerabilities, is a great gift in its own right.

A new vision for who we might be in our relationship with money was cast. We wanted to move from a relationship with money that was vague, aspirational, secretive, duct-taped and bubble gummed together to one that is enough, related, free. We wanted a relationship that had a feeling of a wellspring.

From this space, we began talking with individuals about their own stories, and their own giving to create a new story as a corporate body. People were approached who have never been approached before. Conversations revealed stories that needed voice. People were grateful to be asked. Almost every single person spoken to has increased giving, and done so joyfully. During the corporate trauma of a global health pandemic. And a presidential election.

As was written in their 2020 year-end appeal, "The goals we've set will allow us to write a 2021 budget free from financial dependence on the ELCA. And we'll have resources to be open-hearted and open-handed as we invest in social justice work in our neighborhood, our city, and the world." The idea that shifting where and how money is received will open the congregation up to creativity in ways that they have yet to even know.

St. Lydia's is just one story of the tangled money stories that surround all of our lives and communities. Their continual work to untangle the story, to honor our shared frailty but to also cast a new way, it honors the story given to us by our biblical ancestors.

What is unique about our Christian faith is the belief that newness is consistently being woven amidst the rubble of the world around us. If ever there was a time to bear witness to this it is now.

# CHAPTER TWELVE

# Invested Faith

## *Shifting How We See*

### AMY BUTLER

IT'S A COMMON TRUTH of human living that it all depends on how you see it, and that truth is especially relevant to the church in America today.

One summer when my children were very young our family took a vacation to Rapid City, South Dakota. The vacation was meant to be a memory-making week for eight little cousins, ranging in age from newborn to about five years old.

What we were thinking I will never know.

On the schedule for that week was a visit to Mount Rushmore, that beautiful national memorial carved into the granite face of the mountain. So, we strapped all eight little children into their various car seats, loaded up untold strollers and sippy cups and diaper bags, and took all those kids to visit Mt. Rushmore.

In my memory, it was my sister who had the brilliant idea to stop at the entrance to the memorial visitor center at a vending cart selling ice cream. It was a bright summer day—a great day for ice cream—so all the kids chose their favorite flavors of ice cream, and we sat everybody down so the kids could eat their cones in the hot sunshine.

And eat their ice cream... they did. Well, as much as they could, what with the sun melting it faster than they could lick the drips. There were several of us parents on duty working overtime with napkins, but you might be able to imagine the scene. Little faces and t-shirts, fingers and cheeks—covered—covered, I tell you, with sticky, melted ice cream.

But, we were there to see that memorial, so we got everyone as cleaned up as we could and soldiered on toward the memorial visitors' center. When we got into the visitors' center, there, spread out before us, was a stunning view of the sculpted mountain—framed by a huge pane of clear glass—floor to ceiling glass, looking out over the mountain.

The kids were mesmerized by the view, and they wanted to get as close as they could to see. So they rushed right up to that beautiful glass window and they put their little hands up to reach toward the larger than life sculpture right there in front of them. They exclaimed with excitement and pointed; they leaned their little sticky faces right up against the window to get as close as they could; they slid those little hands up and down the glass as they commented on what they saw.

And me?

Well, I was in a panic.

All of these tourists and monument staff members were watching my children and my nieces and nephews smear that pristine glass window with their excited, little kid reactions to that incredible view.

I wanted nothing other than to get out of there as fast as I could. I began rounding up the kids, pulling them away from the glass. Once we finally had them moving away from the window, I looked back with chagrin at the ice cream smears covering what seemed to me to be the entire bottom third of that glass window.

Down the hill we went, back to the parking lot. We folded the strollers and stashed the diaper bags, strapped everybody into their respective car seats, and hit the road—hoping to get away before anybody at Mt. Rushmore that day could yell at those crazy folks who thought it was a good idea to feed eight children under five ice cream on a hot summer day *right* before they brought them into the Mt. Rushmore visitor center viewing area.

As I drove away I remember a sudden realization: I never saw the monument. I *never* saw the monument. I never stood in silent awe and looked at the masterpiece right in front of me. I never saw the monument!

Here's what I saw. I saw a group of sugar-hyped children—all of whom I love, mind you—smearing melted ice cream on a pristine window, creating an annoyance to other tourists, and leaving a mess. Hyper children, smeared glass, annoyed tourists. That's what I saw. I never even saw the sculpture.

It all depends on how you see it.

According to the Pew Forum on Religion and Public Life, the percentage of Americans who identify as Christian dropped 12% over the last decade. Likewise, the percentage of individuals who attend church monthly or more decreased from 54% to 45% between 2009 and 2019.

Over this same time period, the percentage of "religiously unaffiliated" increased from 17% to 26% of the population, with the group identifying as "nothing in particular" now accounting for 17% of the population (staggering growth, up from 12% in 2009).[1] A theological result of this decline has many congregations across the country spending their time, energy, and resources in pursuit of staving off institutional death, a motivation that is neither compelling nor biblical. Much of American Christianity has allowed the lessons of late-stage capitalism creep into our faith. These values of "bigger is better" and "us vs. them" among others, lead to a deeply embedded theology of scarcity.

I believe that most American Christians go through the motions of tending the institution we call Church—and even our faith

---

1. Pew Research Center, "In U.S., Decline of Christianity Continues at Rapid Pace: An update on America's changing religious landscape," October 17, 2019.

itself—with substantial inattention to the theological assumptions that inform how we behave. As we face a rapidly changing landscape of the institutional church, we must confront this brave new world with an awareness and examination of the theological frameworks we lean on when we're making decisions about how we live our faith in the world.

In short, as we've watched the institutional church steadily decline, we have begun to think and act with a theology of scarcity. God's economy, however, is one built on abundance, possibility, and constant re-creation. Until we adjust the theological lens through which we see our institutional lives we will not be able to find our way into the hopeful future God imagines for us.

This theological framework causes us to shut down, hoard what we have, and turn inward, often at the expense of the most vulnerable among us. We're afraid of losing what has seemed familiar for most of our lives, and we long for an experience of the divine that is perpetually unchanging. Of course, this fear is absolutely reflective of human nature, which craves stasis and generally avoids radical change. But, as Pope Francis reminds us, "Fear is fed and manipulated, because fear—as well as being a good deal for the merchants of arms and death—weakens and destabilizes us, destroys our psychological and spiritual defenses, numbs us to the suffering of others, and in the end it makes us cruel."[2]

Congregations still hold a compelling moral vision for doing good: the vision of the gospel and a holy imagination of a world restored. However, instead of being bold and courageous with these tremendous resources—both theological and financial—too many congregations are preoccupied with the narrative of decline and have defaulted to this theology of scarcity.

By contrast, seeing the world with a biblical theology of abundance is like sitting on the edge of your seat and holding your breath with anticipation for what God is planning next. Looking at the world with a lens of abundance means always allowing the possibility for new winds of God's Spirit. It is the belief that

2. Bailey, "As election nears, Pope Francis warns against fear, building walls" *The Washington Post*, November 6, 2016.

there is enough for everyone to thrive. It is not a belief that all our congregations have enough resources to sustain themselves but that, through abundance, we are able to both innovate and *give away to our neighbors*. People of faith, who see the world this way, walk through life with hands and hearts open, working to love our neighbors generously and to view the stranger with open curiosity and the hope of relationship. A theology of abundance allows us to live, not with a fear of death, but rather boldly and with resurrection hope.

With a theology as people of faith in the world, now is the time to respond to the invitation of God's Spirit with an openness to new ideas and unconventional efforts. One of these projects sits at the intersection of faith, philanthropy, and innovation. The project, Invested Faith, works to embody this theology while working in a new paradigm.

In the course of my work as a pastor and national faith leader, I've noticed two increasing trends: the diminishment of common expressions of congregational life, leading to their subsequent closings, and the rising trend of young church leaders striking out to create "church" in unconventional ways that often do not involve pews and pipe organs. I wondered: where is the generative place in which these two growing realities might meet? This is the impetus of Invested Faith.

We all know that faith institutions in decline often are still stewards of tremendous capital, but the actual data reflecting this is quite mind boggling. According to a 2016 Guardian article, religious institutions and industries in America represent $1.2 trillion a year in wealth. This is more than Apple, Amazon, and Google's combined wealth at the time.[3] This is a huge body of assets that stand to be lost to the work of faith as churches close with no generative options.

Some of the ideas behind Invested Faith were inspired by stories like the Twinbrook Baptist congregation in Rockville, MD that recognized its falling membership and decided that the most

---

3. Sherwood, "Religion in US 'worth more than Google and Apple combined,'" *The Guardian*, September 15, 2016.

faithful use of their remaining resources would be to sell their building, close their doors, and donate $1 million to nonprofits who aligned with their mission. In a *Washington Post* article, Rev. Jill McCrory, the congregation's pastor, shared that "many churches wait until the last minute, and they just dwindle and dwindle and dwindle." Instead, McCrory adds that "shutting down allowed the church to close with dignity."[4]

With congregations willing to be proactive with their assets, I wondered what would happen if we took the idea from a philanthropic exercise to an active investing in the future of faithful witness in the world? We could build a vehicle to receive and invest the assets of sunsetting churches like this so that their history and witness can see a future we can't yet see gospel work being done beyond the stained-glass windows we find so familiar.

Along with the need for new ways churches and other institutions can send their witness forward, people of faith are also confronting the reality that many new faith leaders are answering calls to create new expressions of gospel community outside the walls of the church. In part, they are responding to trends in traditional faith expression. Shifts within the religious landscape in America have left many religious institutions unwilling or unable to take the risks necessary for entrepreneurship and innovation. As a result, in recent years the launch of social enterprises for the common good has often been initiated outside of religious institutions, creating a gap with the traditional church on one side and social entrepreneurs on the other. Increasingly, leaders with theological training are abandoning traditional expressions of professional ministry, but they are still finding their vocations in their communities: launching social enterprises, innovating in contexts beyond the institutional church, and creating new models of community and congregational life.

Invested Faith is one of the efforts stepping into the gap, serving as a bridge between institutional Christianity and social innovation, because this new reality offers a moment in which we can

---

4. Iati, "A liberal Baptist church will close its doors and give $1 million to nonprofits," *The Washington Post*, August 4, 2019.

amplify the exciting convergence of storied history and scrappy innovation.

And while an effort like Invested Faith sounds unfamiliar, it actually builds on a long history of innovation and out-of-the-box thinking by faith communities. When the church was first commissioned Christ sent his disciples out to be the hands and feet of God, to do the work of healing the world, of bringing to life what he called "the kingdom of God." From that time forward, groups of Christians we call the church have been change-makers, innovators, and risk-takers. For example, at the turn of the 19th century churches and faith-based organizations built significant institutions for the purpose of social benefit (think: establishing schools, building the local Baptist hospital, or setting up the YMCA).

By helping communities of faith to reframe the mindset of scarcity toward God's hopeful message of abundance, congregations can thrive through and beyond their traditional institutional lives as they envision how the closing of their institutions might create an opening for a new part of God's story, and likewise, new expressions of gospel community can find the support they need to create the future people of faith are longing to see.

It all depends on how you see it.

In this moment of perceived scarcity, is it possible that God invites us to take risks that align with an alternative economy? Changing our perspective is the first step to embracing the brave new world in which we find ourselves. It also is an act of faith: summoning the courage to follow God's Spirit into the tremendous future that God surely hopes for us all.

*Bibliography:*

Bailey, Sarah Pulliam. "As election nears, Pope Francis warns against fear, building walls." *The Washington Post.* November 6, 2016. https://www.washingtonpost.com/news/acts-of-faith/wp/2016/11/06/as-election-nears-pope-francis-warns-against-fear-building-walls/.

Iati, Marisa. "A liberal Baptist church will close its doors and give $1 million to nonprofits." *The Washington Post.* August 4, 2019. https://www.

washingtonpost.com/religion/2019/08/04/progressive-baptist-church-will-close-its-doors-give-million-nonprofits/.

Pew Research Center, "In U.S., Decline of Christianity Continues at Rapid Pace: An update on America's changing religious landscape," https://www.pewforum.org/2019/10/17/in-u-s-decline-of-christianity-continues-at-rapid-pace/.

Sherwood, Harriet. "Religion in US 'worth more than Google and Apple combined.'" *The Guardian*. September 15, 2016. https://www.theguardian.com/world/2016/sep/15/us-religion-worth-1-trillion-study-economy-apple-google.

# PART V

## Reimagining Wisdom
on the Edge of Uncertainty

# CHAPTER THIRTEEN

# Imagining Belonging with the Book of Acts

## Eric D. Barreto

WE ARE NOT SURE what the future looks like. We are uncertain how and where to discern God's moving in our midst. We are surprised at every turn by the new communities and new stories that we are encountering. We are encumbered by a politics more concerned with the preservation of certain powers and principalities. We are inundated in a politics in which the raw exercise of power matters more than the needs of those most vulnerable. We do not know what is next. Can we trust that God is still with us?

If these sentences seem particularly pressing today, you would be entirely right, of course.

In 2020 in the United States, the intertwined political and theological crises that have haunted communities and churches alike for generations reemerged with fresh power. A worldwide pandemic laid bare truths to which prophets among us had been pointing for generations. A social structure resting on the oppression of others is a crumbling edifice, due for failure. In protests, many voiced old demands rooted in fresh hopes. A different social structure is possible through confession, repair, and reconciliation. The world can be different. Justice is possible.

And yet, I'm struck that the paragraph that began this essay could well have applied in a different context too, one whose stories we encounter as Scripture. In the Acts of the Apostles, Luke narrates such a moment of interlaced crisis and hope. The communities Luke captures in story and speech alike are communities wrestling with the foundation-making forces of empire. Empire carved the social landscape of antiquity, bent the hopes of the communities they ruled around the proliferation and sustenance of empire's desire for acclamation and riches and a purported peace maintained at the edge of a sword.

Too often, however, we have tended to read the Acts of the Apostles as a handbook for building an ideal church, an exacting instruction manual for the ritual and behavior that would make a community of believers quintessentially Christian. I have been convinced that a reading of Acts that looks for such guidance will fall short. Indeed, Acts is not full of instruction and guides for gathering. Instead, Acts teems with story-telling, with fantastic narratives of prison escapes and miracles, shipwrecks and preaching.

And so, I suggest that we turn to the Book of Acts less as a guidebook for putting together a perfect church and more as a spark for our *imaginations*. These stories form us as communities by teaching us something about the character of God, the kinds of promises God makes, and the way that divine character and those divine promises teach us how to belong and commune one with another. But even more, Acts accompanies us in navigating a diverse, complex, challenging world, not so via precise instruction than the prophetic, curious, and hopeful imagination it nurtures in us. With these vibrant stories, we are shaped by what God has done in the past and thus prepared to be formed by the surprising ways God is still moving in our midst. In short, Acts teaches us who God is and precisely in that way nurtures an imagination in us about faithful belonging.

The belonging Acts narrates fuels an imagination about stewardship and philanthropy that can sustain us today. There's a kind of insipid hope in too many churches today that is rooted in privilege and luck, a vapid hope that rests on "happy" accidents that accrue to a community and which are mistaken for blessing. Such hope is brittle, for it fails at the first encounter with difficulty. Instead, Acts narrates truer, richer, more vibrant hope that drives toward faithful belonging. Acts teaches us a belonging nurtured in the struggles of everyday life. Acts narrates a belonging in a way that seeks to shape our yearnings for precisely such belonging.

Very briefly then, let's look at three insights into imaginations faithful belonging that Acts narrates, three characteristics of a community that yearns for God's grace. Such faithful belonging in light of God's grace is a scriptural ground upon which we can reimagine how faith in God and philanthropy infused with such faith might nourish transformative, life-giving community.

## 1. Difference is a Gift

Faithful belonging proliferates and embraces difference. Many readings of Pentecost see in the proliferation of tongues by the Spirit a reversal of the Tower of Babel in Genesis 11, a deliverance from the thorny problems of many languages, many peoples, many cultures. Such a reading assumes that our differences are a problem our faith can solve, that the very existence of different cultures is a curse lingering from the arrogance of the inhabitants of Babel. This is a misreading of Babel and Pentecost alike. Instead, notice that the Spirit speaks through the disciples in all the languages of the world, in all their strange syntax and vocabulary. God does not ask us to learn a new language to hear good news. Instead, God draws near to us precisely at that place where difference proliferates. Community flourishes when we embrace particularity and difference precisely because this is God's creative design for our lives together.

## 2. Community is a Matter of Life and Death

At the same time, faithful belonging is fragile. Here we turn to the beginning of Acts 5. In the wake of the utopian description of a community where need had ceased (Acts 4:32-37), the story of Ananias and Sapphira is sobering. Even in the earliest days of the church, utopian unity was fleeting. Here, we do not see a model for how to deal with deception in community, but a glimpse into the high stakes of life lived together. The stakes are high because community is a matter of life and death. What if churches started understanding their belonging not just as social nicety or network, but as the very site of God's resurrection activity in our midst? That is, when we gather to worship, eat, live together, we are holding each other's lives in our hands. And thus community is both vital *and* fragile. Community must be carefully nurtured, and we must turn to the generous character of God to embody that fragile *and* faithful belonging. We might even call this a faithfully fragile belonging.

## 3. The Empire is Crumbling from Within

Faithful belonging bears witness to the crumbling of empire. In Acts 12:20-23, Luke includes an aside about Herod's arrogant claim to power and his embrace of divine acclamation from a people desperate for his assistance. As the people declare, "The voice of a god, and not of a mortal!," Herod is struck down; "he was eaten by worms and died" (v. 23, NRSV). Empire is devoured from within by its arrogance, drowned by the false claims to divine power, crumbles under the weight of the injustices it perpetrates. Empire is crumbling from within. Let me be clear. Faithful belonging does not cause the downfall of empire; that is solely the work of God. Yet faithful belonging embodies a truth empire wishes to deny. Empire's power is but a pale imitation of the kind of power faithful belonging reflects.

These three are but only a few insights into faithful belonging Acts might inspire in us. Many more could be added. So, let me gesture towards one last characteristic of transformative community. As we reach the end of its pages, the end of Acts leaves the reader hanging a bit. The book ends unexpectedly noting that Paul, though in chains and awaiting his execution, is preaching the good news without hindrance. Unencumbered, without hindrance. Not unconnected or unconcerned. The last image we see in Acts is a Paul imprisoned, yes, but also liberated, empowered, and transformed by the good news that God has promised to set the world right and is already doing so in the communities that gather around Jesus' name.

I wonder if American Christianity has nurtured in too many a sense that the everyday of life does not matter much, that the results of an election are as momentous as the victor of a football game, that God's deliverance in the end means that the suffering of some in the meantime pales in comparison to the promised victory. Belonging teaches us otherwise. The loving embrace of the stories of others liberates us from an assumption that we are observers of the suffering and courage of others and brings us to a proximity and a participation that draws us close to our neighbors.

Belonging is a vital word for Christians as we seek to emerge in a faithful way from the various crises that will ensure 2020 is seared in our memories. In a world riven by division, God calls God's children to nurture belonging, a place and a people among which we know we are welcomed and embraced. Peter Block puts it this way: "Belonging can also be thought of as a longing to be. Being is our capacity to find our deeper purpose in all that we do. It is the capacity to be present, and to discover our authenticity and whole selves. This is often thought of as an individual capacity, but it is also a community capacity. Community is the container within which our longing to be is fulfilled. Without the connectedness of a community, we will continue to choose not to be."[1]

Belonging is a feeling: a longing for a place and a people to call home. Belonging is a hope: a yearning for home that is ever more expansive and diverse. Belonging is a prophetic act: an embodied declaration that communities can be a beacon of God's

1. Block, *Community*, xii.

justice. Belonging is imagination: a transformative vision of a world turned upside by a God who reigns in justice and grace.

We must also distinguish carefully between belonging and possession. The former is a movement of the Spirit that draws us into wholeness and love. The latter is a distortion of the created order, a claiming to own peoples and lands and stuff that actually belong to God. Belonging excludes the demonic possession that teaches us the world is ours to grasp rather than a gift we share for the sake of others. In addition, faithful belonging invites us all to participate and be in community in all the fulness of our rich identities and thus excludes the all-too-common requirement that minoritized people sacrifice their identities and even their bodies for the sake of a community seeking to diversify. That is, even in the good striving towards a more faithful belonging, we must fight the temptation to possess the identities and bodies of the minoritized as mere means towards an end. Too often, majority cultures in the church have sought to possess minoritized bodies, to objectify them as evidence of progress. Instead, belonging is not possessive or possessed. Belonging, faithful belonging, means holding each other's lives as precious gifts of God.

Belonging, in short, reminds us who and whose we are. We belong to God and thus one to another. And in this way, faithful belonging can reorient our sense of stewardship, re-root what Christian philanthropy might be in a world in need of repair. We give and share as a practice of belonging, a practice that proliferates difference, that takes seriously the high stakes of communal life, that points to the sharp contrast between empire's arrogations and the grace of God's reign.

### Bibliography:

Block, Peter. *Community: The Structure of Belonging.* San Francisco: Berrett-Kohler, 2008.

# CHAPTER FOURTEEN

# Everything Is An Experiment

## Sunia Gibbs

"I cannot go in these," he said to Saul, "because I am not used to them." So he took them off. Then he took his staff in his hand, chose five smooth stones from the stream, put them in the pouch of his shepherd's bag and, with his sling in his hand, approached the Philistine."

1 SAMUEL 17:39–40 (NIV)

"Everything is an experiment. I have the right to fail and try again. I will bring my whole self into the work. I will not assimilate."

(THE SPEECH I GIVE MYSELF EVERY SINGLE DAY.)

BEFORE I AM ANYTHING, I am an artist, flowing as a songwriter and abstract painter. Whatever enters through my senses, processes as a feeling and emerges a lyric or brush stroke. The beginning of every creative work is inspiration and curiosity. The middle, in the plodding thick of it, is bravery. And the end is pure commitment. Usually an image or word will grab my attention and begin bouncing around in my mind, body, and heart, looking for a connection and a way to be expressed. Those initial moments of output are exhilarating and liberating. But following very quickly is perfectionistic fear. What if the next color I add ruins this whole painting? What if this song is the wrong tempo, vibe, or message? What if *I* am wrong? I have literally stood in front of my work repeating to myself, "be brave, be brave, be brave" then rationally reminding myself that gesso and "command Z" erase every error. In my particular process, I have learned to not discard, that each attempt actually adds texture and nuance, beauty. It's the layers of a work's history that lead to the moment I can step back and say, "It is good."

Then I am released.

I remember when I stepped into my current role as an executive director and pastor, and, for a moment, felt the pressure to become the white male CEO business model type leader I had always experienced. Systematic. Solution-driven. Hierarchical. I was David trying on Saul's armor and sword to fight Goliath. None of it fit, even when I really wanted it to. And while acknowledging what didn't work was important, discovering what authentically does became deep, internal work that had life changing implications.

In this very moment, as an Asian-American artist, pastor, and activist, I am responding to an adamant inner voice and a growing external demand to be an integrated, intersectional leader. Discovering the gifts and necessary tools are already present within me, I am able to adapt and shift. This is not in frantic, compromised assimilation but with clarity and confidence navigating in the midst of the unknown and unpredictable.

Arguably, traditional, linear, often compartmentalized approaches to ministry and faith-life have not been adequate to address the complexities and nuances of the world we live in. I have been invited to trust in the Divinely placed intersections I embody, being liberated and refusing to fall back into old patterns, even when it would be much, much easier. I can risk something new, something I haven't tried before and not execute it perfectly. As an artist I make mistakes. So too as a pastor, so too as an organizational leader, so too as a partner and mother. And on and on.

I should note this is not a process I learned through my formal education, internships, or leadership books. I thought I was leading for a very long time, though I was actually just really good at copying and people-pleasing. (Model minority, assimilation, Asian-American life.) I identified that when those in charge are flattered through mimicry, and their needs are centered, they offer microphones, stage time—and even jobs. I performed and managed in exchange for platforms, privileges, and pay.

This was particularly compromising and soul-crushing as a creative artist in church life. My songs were inappropriate—"We don't talk about those things," someone shared—or too sad—"We want to encourage people," another responded—or not enough JPS's (Jesus per seconds). My art was abstract and didn't make sense: "Maybe if there was a cross in there," a viewer wondered. So I stuck to the standards and performed, climbed the ladder, reaching boredom and the proverbial glass (or bamboo) ceiling.

Eventually, I left my paid ministry life and wandered. I cried a lot because deserts are truly isolated and barren! But eventually the dissatisfaction that led to the wilderness brought me back into the parish, into the neighborhood where I found new conversations, concerns, and perspectives. I started writing new kinds of songs. I began to imagine faith-life beyond existing institutional structures, centering people otherwise ignored or unseen. Many of the ideas and dreams of the integrated life and work I am currently experimenting with came in that season.

The good news is contextual. This means paying attention, listening, and taking note of what is happening around me, particularly in, with and around marginalized people. Jesus did, after all, come to bring good news to the poor and set the oppressed free. I am learning to be brave with whatever power and privilege I (we) hold in order to participate in the liberating work of Jesus in our neighborhood.

Two significant, personal experiences forced me to consider the intersections of leadership and race. First, one of only two black men in our congregation was tragically shot and killed by police on our university campus. The distance I once had from gun violence and communities of color was removed as I was confronted with my own place and privilege. Cops weren't killing black men over there in that *other* city, but in my own neighborhood, to my friend, in my church. How was I as an Asian female to lead and pastor in this moment? How do we show up for a family destroyed by racism and police violence?

Second, our family adopted a black-white bi-racial child. I began to recognize the differences in parenting between him and my older Asian-American children. How does a Korean adoptee and a man of English/Welch descent raise a healthy black man in a very white city?

I was no longer allowed to be a bystander or adjacent. This invitation was to life-long engagement, adaptation, and advocacy.

As I came to increasingly identify as a Korean-American, I intentionally began seeking, learning and leading with other persons of color, gathering and drawing others into the work of anti-racism. The questions, mentoring, and growth have led me to begin to center our work for and with BIPOC and marginalized persons.

An outsider who learned to assimilate in order to fit in, I am particularly drawn towards those who have been excluded and deep admiration for those who have refused to compromise their identity in order to show up. I want to lead with them.

Everything is an experiment; none of us have ever done this before. We need permission (and funding) to try and fail. We have to throw paint on the canvas, write melodies for our lyrics, and put our theories into practice. They might not work. But we can grow, and learn, and maybe even innovate and create beauty along the way.

I am currently moving my congregation and organization towards being a multi-ethnic faith community. This requires full participation and shared power. We are developing literacy and language, exploring partnerships and ways of structuring, trying and failing and trying again, making mistakes and trusting all will contribute to the beauty of who we are becoming. We have long discussions and work through misunderstandings and miscommunication. Some people have decided to walk away. Others have joined in. I paint and write and sing about it. I fall short and we get closer every day.

I hope the work we are doing is liberation. I hope it is deeply personal and thoroughly, significantly structural and communal.

The invitation to lead did not come with a clear path or destination, but a promise of presence and a hope to see kin-dom realities in unexpected places. Faith and trust are key. If I forget the character of God, if I doubt God's goodness and lose hope, the barrenness of the wilderness will tempt me to go back to Egypt—or wander, and focus on something I've created. If I forget the words, life, death, and resurrection of Jesus, I'll lose sight of how and why I'm in this work. If I am not attentive, empowered, and guided by God's Spirit, I will lack the strength to persevere.

For those who see my work as an artist, musician, or communicator, I hope there is increased freedom to lead beyond the creative sphere. I hope that we imagine our creative selves leading faith communities and organizations, sitting on neighborhood, city, and school boards, contributing our work and our way of being and thinking.

As I navigate these unprecedented times, sheltering in place during a global pandemic, protesting in the streets with masks and hand sanitizer, I'm hopeful. For the first time I feel like I was made for this moment—that who I am and what I offer is precisely what we need right now.

# CHAPTER FIFTEEN

# A Time of Rustling

## Ecclesial Ecologies on the Edge of Uncertainty

### Dustin D. Benac

CROSSING A LEAF-STREWN YARD in the Pacific Northwest, I paused for a moment to look upward into the kaleidoscope of colors. Orange and yellowing maple leaves stand suspended, tied to life with delicate threads. As the wind lifts a leaf from where it rests, breaking the ties that bind, it flies blown and tossed by the wind. Its solitary form looks fragile against a pale-grey morning sky, giving silent protest to an impending and inescapable fall from the elevated place it once stood.

It is a time of rustling.

As a practical theologian who studies religious organizations, I have come to the Pacific Northwest to study how networks of religious organizations are adapting to uncertain circumstances. Even as religious organizations in the Pacific Northwest occupy a marginal social position, they carry on a legacy of entrepreneurship. "It is in the water we drink," one leader shares. New partnerships, in particular, provide place and space to imagine how to reorder a common life anew.

This broader ecclesial ecology also bears witness to an imagination that is brimming with endless possibilities.

In this pre-COVID-19 moment, however, my inquiry imbibes uncertainty in ways that border on recklessness: I have left my family, including a twenty-month-old son and gestating daughter, flown more than two thousand miles, and all for a conversation that is not confirmed. I carry these sacred memories and bonds of care, even as I hope for a future that I cannot see. Like so many others who now walk on the edge of uncertainty, memories of these dear ones are always close at hand.

Pausing anxiously for a moment outside this door—uncertain whether to enter or retreat—I knock and then enter, crossing the threshold of certainty.

Religion in the Pacific Northwest provides a case to consider the forms of imagination that can sustain faith communities in this time of rustling. For example, in 1914 E. J. Klemme speculated that the Great Divide "seemed too steep for church letters" and "the air of the Northwest seemed too rare for prayer."[1] Patricia Killen aptly describes the region as the "canary in the mine" about the "the consciousness and conscience of humanity."[2] More recently, Mark Silk characterizes the region as "the American religious future."[3] These descriptions paint a fairly consistent picture: religious organizations in the region, much like the single leaf I mentioned, are fragile, occupying a marginal social position in a shifting institutional landscape.

In the Pacific Northwest, much as for faith communities across the United States, adaptive challenges confront every sector of a shifting ecclesial ecology. Congregations, nonprofits, theological education, faith-based philanthropy, church-plants, and ecclesial innovations all feel the winds of change. While each community faces contextually-specific challenges, this moment raises systems-level challenges. The various challenges, fragilities, and

1. E. J. Klemme, in *The Pacific Northwest Pulpit*, quoted in Killen, "Introduction," 9.

2. Killen, "Memory," 83–85.

3. Silk, "The Pacific Northwest is the American religious future."

possibilities are shared across an ecclesial ecology, such that discerning faith-filled ways forward requires attending the challenges and networks that cross sectors, providing spaces for connection, resistance, and creativity.

I have come to attend to a changing ecclesial ecology.

Following my first unconfirmed conversation, which goes well, momentum builds, sparking conversations across the region. I interview pastors, nonprofit leaders, students, college presidents, deans, philanthropists, and parachurch workers over the next three years. And as I listen to leaders and people of faith across this ecology, I hear consistent challenges: relational engagement, leadership development, a post-Christian context, loneliness, financial stability, caring for a church in transition, the complexity of partnership, racial injustice. Indeed, these are adaptive issues; each represents challenges that lack a clear solution and require collective effort to achieve change.

But beneath this descriptive gloss, these leaders and their communities share a more fundamental feature: a collective, contextual imagination is rising to renew a broader ecclesial ecology. In this time of rustling, we need a new way of seeing. We need new ways of belonging. We need ways of mending polarizing communities. We need winsome wisdom to incarnate the story of God in the communities we serve. We need new ways to imagine and craft a common life.

Three features of this changing ecclesial ecology can guide collective efforts to (re)imagine a common life in times of rustling.

First, an ecclesial ecology serves as a *place* that fosters and nourishes imagination to respond to the challenges that communities face. The formation and exercise of imagination literally *takes place*. It forms in the space between established and emerging forms of ecclesial life: congregations, educational institutions, and theological schools provide language to apprehend and navigate the life of faith. Meanwhile, encounters in families, neighborhoods, and friendship provide the social matrix for this kind of imagination to find its form and function.

In this time of rustling, we need new imagination to see the latent possibilities in the various places we inhabit.

The particularities of place foster a contextually-attentive imagination, one that carries the stories of our communities, and a connective imagination in order to partner across the various places where faith forms. When combined, leadership and communities express wisdom that attends to the particularities of place in order to incarnate Christ's connective presence in the communities we serve. In this moment of rustling, the (re)formation of imagination is literally taking place.

Second, an ecclesial ecology provides a *prism*, redirecting individual and collective imagination. Like light shined through a triangular prism, participation in an ecclesial ecology clarifies and redirects the imagination that may respond to the challenges we face. In countless instances, individuals shared how their participation across this ecclesial ecology contributed to "transformation." Encounters in neighborhoods, friendships that span decades, mentors from college, co-journeyers in bible study and reading groups. In ordinary and mundane ways, these are sites of encounter that clarify how to live in light of the reality and possibilities of God.

Participation in this ecclesial ecology also redirects imagination. The challenges that confront communities of faith—within and beyond the Pacific Northwest—invite a change of course. As one leader shared, "[We] know the current models aren't working .... Everybody recognizes that there are challenges, that we don't control these factors." Or, as another leader expressed more poignantly, "Our colonial, Christendom idea of church ... is non-existence." In each case, relational encounters provide sites to (re) form a kind of imagination that is nimble and adaptive.

In this time of rustling, it is not time to go it alone. Rather, partnerships, friendship, and collaboration provide the imaginative sustenance to pursue the adaptive work change requires. In the face of complex and pernicious challenges, especially ones that diminish our collective humanity, we need to see the imaginative possibilities that exist on the edge of uncertainty. We need relational and institutional space to clarify and redirect our individual and collective imagination.

This introduces a third feature of this changing ecclesial ecology: philanthropy supports the conditions where new imagination may form and flourish. Philanthropy describes a way of life marked by generosity, including the ability to give *and* be received by others, in order to enrich the common good.[4] As an ecclesial ecology responds to shifting landscape, wisdom borne of conventional and grassroots approaches to philanthropy flows through this ecology.

Conventional approaches to philanthropy allocate resources, make connections, and steward the institutional memory that can sustain adaptive change. Grassroots approaches to philanthropy remain nimble, responding to the local needs of communities, and tending to the local connections that comprise an ecclesial ecology.

We need both approaches. Like blood pulsing through our veins, the wisdom of conventional and grassroots approaches to philanthropy open space for the connection, care, and resourcing that people of faith so desperately need. And like the systolic and diastolic beating of a heart, these two modes of philanthropy release words, wisdom, and care to a world in need. When combined and coordinated, this twin approaches to philanthropy influences how individuals and communities reimagine their common life.

In this time of rustling, these three features are intertwined in a virtuous pattern of interdependence. The placed, prismatic, and philanthropic qualities combine to enrich an imagination that may bend an ecclesial ecology toward more life-giving possibilities. When segmented or pursued apart from the others, our individual and collective imagination diminishes. Ecclesial ecologies become less vibrant and less adaptive when we fail to attend to how these three features may support change within our local communities.

Naming this interrelationship does not lessen the challenges that confront communities of faith. For some, this time of rustling feels disruptive in ways that bring grief, loss, and pain. For others,

---

4. See Tempel, Seiler, and Burlingame, eds. *Achieving Excellence in Fundraising* and Jeavons, *When the Bottom Line is Faithfulness.*

it breaks open new possibilities as established norms yield to new horizons.

We exist in a suspended state, one marked by uncertainty, change, and possibility. This state is neither new nor novel; it reflects what we have always been, and always will be. To borrow a phrase from Langston Hugh, communities of faith "yet must be" places of hope, equity, peace, and care.[5]

In this moment, as we look upward beneath the changing foliage that adorns our communities, we exit in a time of rustling that invites new imagination. This imagination emerges when these placed, prismatic, and philanthropic qualities of our ecclesial ecologies meet and mingle. It takes form when leaders and communities of faith come to see the interconnectedness that binds us together. It rises as we join together, in virtuous patterns of giving and belonging, living into the yet-ness that marks our individual and ecclesial imagination.

## Bibliography:

Hughes, Langston. "Let American be American Again." *The Collected Poems of Langston Hughes*. Edited by Arnold Rampersad. New York: Vintage Classics, 1994.

Jeavons, Thomas. *When the Bottom Line is Faithfulness: Management of Christian Service* Organizations. Bloomington: Indiana University Press, 1994.

Killen, Patricia. "Introduction—Patterns of the Past, Prospects for the Future: Religion in the None Zone." In *Cascadia: The Elusive Utopia: Exploring the Spirit of the Pacific Northwest*, edited by Douglas Todd, 9–20. Vancouver: Ronsdale, 2008.

———. "Memory, Novelty and Possibility in this Place." In *Cascadia: The Elusive Utopia: Exploring the Spirit of the Pacific Northwest*, edited by Douglas Todd, 65–85. Vancouver: Ronsdale, 2008.

5. Langston Hughes, "Let America Be American Again," 191. The surrounding lines read: "O, let America be America again— / The land that never has been yet— /
And yet must be—the land where *every* man is free."

Klemme, E. J. *The Pacific Northwest Pulpit*. Compiled by Paul Little. New York: The United Methodist Book Concern, 1915.

Tempel, Eugene, Timothy Seiler and Dwight Burlingame, eds. *Achieving Excellence in Fundraising*. 4th ed. Hoboken, NJ: Wiley & Sons, 2016.

Silk, Mark. "The Pacific Northwest is the American religious future." *Religious News Service*. June 4, 2019.

CONCLUSION

# What Do These Stones Mean?

DUSTIN D. BENAC

ERIN WEBER-JOHNSON

*Now comes the time of endings. For centuries all of our cultures*
*have marked it. It is the fallow season, the time when the Earth*
*sleeps. Its beauty is a stillness, a quietness that settles over life*
*like snowfall and brings all things to their completion before the*
*regeneration of Spring. Therefore this is a profound moment*
*to consider those things in our lives that we need to bring to a*
*close. In each of us there are the loose ends of life, the wear built*
*up over years of hard use. Bad memories, old arguments, lost*
*chances, hurt feelings, family disputes: now is the season to do a*
*little spiritual inventory, to find those loose ends, and to let go of*
*what we do not need to carry into the next chapter of our story.*
*Let that part of the past stay here.*

—THE RT. REV. STEPHEN CHARLESTON[1]
CHOCTAW ELDER, RETIRED BISHOP OF ALASKA

1. Charleston. *Daily Meditations.*

WHILE RECENTLY RECOVERING FROM the COVID-19, Erin received a care package with a postcard on which were printed the words, "The wilderness does not last forever... God is with us in the wilderness." Not unlike the wilderness of the Exodus, the wilderness of the COVID-19 pandemic time is shot through with grief, exhaustion, and a pervading sense of uncertainty. Yet, like the biblical wilderness, as the preceding chapters reveal, our collective experience of this time comes with startling encounters with God's presence and provision, a delightful rekindling of imagination and creativity, and the profound reminder that in and through it all we belong to and with each other.

The presidential elections of 2016 and 2020 provided bookends for this project. Even as uncertainty and fatigue mark our lives beyond this time, communities of faith have faced cascading crises of unpredictability, transition, and loss during this time. Four years ago on election night, we went to bed unsure of what the days would bring. Four years later, these feelings have deepened at times to exhaustion and anger when intersecting with civil rights unrest, economic uncertainty, and our own mortality. Even as we write this, the 2020 election is still being litigated more than a month after Election Day, and the path forward for our nation seems unclear. So too, the church is shifting. A growing percentage of seminary graduates are pursuing ministry beyond a full-time congregational setting.[2] Educational institutions face prevailing headwinds.[3] Local congregations find themselves at missional intersections.[4] It is a time of rustling.

In Joshua 4:5-7 we read: "Joshua said to them: 'Cross over before the ark of the Lord your God into the midst of the Jordan, and each of you take up a stone on his shoulder, according to the number of the tribes of the children of Israel, that this may be a sign among you when your children ask in time to come, saying, 'What do these stones mean to you?' Then you shall answer them

2. Scharen and Campbell-Reed. "Learning Pastoral Imagination."

3. Simon, "We Must Own Our Own Futures."

4. Benac and Weber-Johnson. "Ecclesial Imagination for Organizational Transformation."

that the waters of the Jordan were cut off before the ark of the covenant of the Lord; when it crossed over the Jordan, the waters of the Jordan were cut off. And these stones shall be for a memorial to the children of Israel forever" (NKJV).

Joshua's narrative recounts a decisive moment in the Israelites' journey, one marked by transition and uncertainty. We read of how Moses calls the people of God out of an economy of slavery. Walter Brueggemann writes, "For good reason the emancipated slaves had an urging to return to the desire system of Pharaoh that had victimized them. Since Pharaoh had monopolized all the food they were left with wonderment whether there would be any viable alternative to the system of Pharaoh."[5] For 40 years, burdened by decades of trauma and informed by the commodification of their bodies, they wandered. Moses led his people in the wilderness, still bearing the psychic and physical wounds from their long experience of systematic oppression and the brutality of an empire. Ultimately, he does not cross over to what comes next.

As a generation of the people of God lived and died in the wilderness, so too the Israelites own collective identity was being remade and a new leader emerged. It is in this context that Joshua is charged with leading a people at the intersection of *crisis* and *care*. And as the people cross over the Jordan, they are tasked to make sense of the stones they carry with them.

The story of this transition—from Moses to Joshua, from one generation to another, the wrestling with and reshaping of a people's identity—enlivens our imagination as we listen anew to the wisdom of the authors in this book. The contributions to this volume give language and shape to our imaginations. Standing on the threshold of the post-2020 presidential election, we are invited to consider how to cross over in our own contexts. In so doing, we reread this scene of the pivotal season of transition in Joshua. Joshua inherits the task, as Kevin Kim Wright might describe it, to receive the generosity of death. Or, using the lens provided by Emily Hull McGee, one could say the people were mindful that the time had come to put away "former things."

5. Brueggemann, *Money and Possessions*, 21.

In our haste to find resolution and the comfort of stability, it might be easy to brush past the "crossing over" moment in the narrative. We like to know the end and, so, our imaginations are reluctant to linger in this moment of liminality, rushing instead to the outcome. But, the narrative seems to linger here, pausing to note the manner in which they are to cross over. Joshua invites a newly constituted people to cross the river into a new land, and on the way charges each of the leaders of the twelve tribes to pick up a stone from the river. They are to carry these river rocks with them as weighty markers—as a memorial. And, in fact, these are to be a sign provoking future generations, to ask "What do these stones mean?"

Just as children will ask about Passover so they can hear the story of deliverance from slavery in Egypt (Exod 12:26-27), so they will ask about these stones and hear how God dried up the waters of the Jordan River and their safe passage across (Josh 4:23).[6] They will recount the losses and the grief. They will remember the systems they chose to reject. They will recount how God delivered them from the crises of flood and famine. They will remember God's faithfulness time after time and, in so doing, reclaim their collective identity as children of God.

In creating this volume, we sought to mark the past four years as a time of crossing over. Yet, in the midst of the transition, we still do not know what the days ahead will hold. Even as we write this the death toll caused by COVID-19 continues to climb dramatically, breaking grim new records, and as news of vaccines speed our way it is yet unclear when the shadow of pandemic will leave us. And, yet, drawn forward by hope, we continue to cross over.

What do these stones mean? How do we mark this time of "crossing over"?

As editors we sought to explore these questions, to provide space for imagination and creativity to flourish. This book was created to give voice to where new forms of being and belonging have emerged these past four years.

6. Whitefield, *Commentary on Joshua 5: 9-12*, para 5–7.

The wisdom shared by the contributors to this book speak to a new way of being both ourselves and in being together. Authors spoke to the power that comes with naming who we are, in this moment. Sunia Gibbs, began her chapter with this powerful mantra: "Everything is an experiment. I have the right to fail and try again. I will bring my whole self into the work. I will not assimilate." Mieke Vandersall demonstrates how matters of money and philanthropy shape how we imagine possibility in moments of crisis: "Ecclesial innovation takes place in the site of rupture between our inherited money stories and the alternative economy Scripture outlines." In seen and unseen ways, finance and faith are twin fulcrums for imagination.

Yet, if there is a challenge not only to the church but to our society as a whole in this present moment, it is the challenge of connection. It seems almost cliché to opine about the divisions we face in our world today, yet, those divisions are sharp and they are real. The chapters you have just read were composed and written before and during one of the most divisive elections seasons in memory, yet even now we hear calls for reconciliation and unity. What does unity look like? What might healing our divisions mean? Lawsuits over the outcome of this election are (at the time of this writing) still ongoing. We witnessed the weeks of protests and uprisings all over the country following the murder of George Floyd and experienced the pain of unmet justice. And even as we finalize this conclusion, we've watched with horror as fires of distrust burned at our Capitol on January 6, 2021, incited by a sitting president and a white nationalist mob.[7]

While the reality of crisis is not new, the draconian distrust that divides individuals in the time marked by this volume has the capacity to desiccate the fabric of care within our communities. In this volume, authors already were giving witness to these times. Eric Barreto in writing about a reimagined belonging notes, "Belonging is a prophetic act: an embodied declaration that

---

7. As Whitehead and Perry observe, the fusion of Christianity with American civic life provides a rationale for Christian nationalism in the United States (Whitehead and Perry, *Taking America Back for God*, 10).

communities can be a beacon of God's justice." What is reconciliation, racial, political, and economic, to mean in the midst of these realities?

The answers that come to these and many more questions will require, as we hope this book models, time and space and an imagination enlivened by the story of God and God's people alive and at work in the world. Again, as we hope you have read, the answers will not be easy or simple but full of the complexity of a humanity wrestling to survive amidst a world often at odds with itself.

Sustainable change requires making space for people to speak across traditional boundaries and institutional silos into a space that values collaboration and innovation. It is these partnerships, as authors repeatedly demonstrated, in these times that have renewed our understanding of interconnectedness. The contextual engagement in this volume demonstrates the latent possibilities and complexity of this type of interconnectedness at the insurrection of faith and philanthropy. Shannon Hopkins and Mark Sampson's chapter invites us to reimagine economics within a shared mutuality. Even as this theme intersects with Amy Butler's introduction of Invested Faith, her wisdom shows how we need eyes to see where the broader ecology takes place. Like the imagery of a musical fugue, the push and pull of these chapters intentionally provides an unfinished quality of the conversation.

What do these stones mean? How do we mark this time of "crossing over"?

These stones we carry, these chapters, mark our grief. They give space for listening, for testifying to our deaths, and remembering our profound losses.

We are still in a time of suffering and grief; we grieve what we have lost in political discourse, those who have died in the pandemic, and previous imaginations of the church. Recently, a friend lost his father to COVID-19. He conveyed how bewildering it was to grieve without the ability to gather and practice our "customs of comfort." As we mark a time of crossing over, we long for these customs of comfort, but they frequently feel fleeting or out of reach. How will we mark this season of upending and grief?

As the people of God crossed over the Jordan, we too will mark this time with stones—stones that bear witness to our struggle, that bear witness to our humanity, that give witness to thousands of deaths from institutional racism, a terrible pandemic, and our inability to care for one another.

We will mark this time with the stones of memory and story. Aimée Laramore once noted that we often are quick to think of philanthropy as the 3 t's: time, treasure, and talent. In doing so we leave out a crucial act of faith and philanthropy: the power of testifying to our story of God in the world.

We mark in these chapters the ways we have survived and reclaimed our identity as the people of God. As poet Lucille Clifton writes:

> won't you celebrate with me
> what i have shaped into
> a kind of life? I had no model.
> born in babylon
> both nonwhite and woman
> what did i see to be except myself?
> i made it up
> here on this bridge between
> starshine and clay,
> my one hand holding tight
> my other hand; come celebrate
> with me that everyday
> something has tried to kill me
> and has failed.[8]

What do these stones mean?

Like the stones, there is an unfinished quality to our conversation in this volume. We are a people on the way. We are crossing while also building new systems and ways of being with one another. As Patrick Reyes beautifully describes, "Adaptation is

---

8. Clifton, *The Book of Light*, 25.

honoring those generations of survival while building the world I want that young woman in five generations to inherit."

As we stand "on the bridge between starshine and clay," we recover new images and new language in the stories of those that have come before us. We imagine new economies and ways of being with and for one another. We kindle hopeful imagination in our communities. When exploring faith and philanthropy, we remember we belong to one another.

In a moment of transition, as we linger in the space of crossing over, ecclesial imagination arises where crises and care converge.

## *Bibliography:*

Benac, Dustin D. and Erin Weber-Johnson. "Ecclesial Imagination for Organizational Transformation: Hospice Care, Midwifery, and the Ordering of a Common life." *Practical Theology* 12:2, (2019): 158-174.

Brueggemann, Walter. *Money and Possessions: Interpretation Resources for Use of Scripture in the Church.* Louisville: Westminster John Knox, 2016.

Charleston, Stephen. *Daily Meditations,* December 10, 2020. https://www.redmoonpublications.com/.

Clifton, Lucille. *The Book of Light.* Port Townsend, WA: Copper Canyon, 1993.

Scharen, Christian and Eileen Campbell-Reed. "Learning Pastoral Imagination: A Five-Year Report on How New Ministers Learn in Practice." *Auburn Studies,* no. 21 (winter 2016): 1-64. http://pastoralimagination.com/wp-content/uploads/2016/03/CSTE-LPI-030116.pdf.

Simon, John. "We Must Own Our Own Futures." *Inside Higher Ed.* September 24, 2019. https://www.insidehighered.com/views/2019/09/24/three-major-categories-change-colleges-will-have-deal-coming-decades-opinion.

Whitefield, Bryan J. *Commentary on Joshua 5: 9-12. Working Preacher.* March 31, 2019. https://www.workingpreacher.org/commentaries/revised-common-lectionary/fourth-sunday-in-lent-3/commentary-on-joshua-59-12-4.

Whitehead, Andrew and Samuel Perry. *Taking America Back for God: Christian Nationalism in the United States.* Oxford: Oxford University Press, 2020.

Made in the USA
Monee, IL
21 October 2021

80513737R10100